IT'S YOUR MOVE

by Chris Ward

Published by Everyman Publishers plc London

First published in 2000 by Everyman Publishers plc, formerly Cadogan Books plc, Gloucester Mansions, 140A Shaftesbury Avenue, London WC2H 8HD

Reprinted 2002

British Library Cataloguing-in-Publication Data
A catalogue record for this book is available from the British Library.

ISBN 1 85744 296 2

Distributed in North America by The Globe Pequot Press, P.O Box 480, 246 Goose Lane, Guilford, CT 06437-0480.

All other sales enquiries should be directed to Everyman Chess, Gloucester Mansions, 140A Shaftesbury Avenue, London WC2H 8HD
tel: 020 7539 7600 fax: 020 7379 4060
email: dan@everyman.uk.com
website: www.everyman.uk.com

EVERYMAN CHESS SERIES (formerly Cadogan Chess)
Chief Advisor: Garry Kasparov
Advisory Panel: Andrew Kinsman and Byron Jacobs

Typeset and edited by First Rank Publishing, Brighton.
Production by Book Production Services.
Printed and bound in Great Britain by The Cromwell Press Ltd., Trowbridge, Wiltshire.

Contents

Introduction   5

Test One   8

Test Two   28

Test Three   48

Test Four   68

Test Five   88

Test One - Solutions   108

Test Two - Solutions   115

Test Three - Solutions   122

Test Four - Solutions   129

Test Five - Solutions   136

Marking Scheme and Scorechart   143

Introduction

Welcome to *It's Your Move* where, well, it's your move! However, you are not alone as in a variation on usual multiple-choice texts, you are being offered advice from our panel of ... Well, perhaps not experts(!), but occasionally our characters have some good ideas and for sure in each question that you are asked, one of them has just the plan that was successfully employed by a strong player in a real game. It's your task to discern which of our loveable characters has the best continuation in mind from a given position and I guess now is the time for you to meet them.

Introducing The Characters

'Ambitious' Andy
Not even the sky's the limit for Andy who frequently sets his sights beyond the ozone layer! Ultra-confident in all he does, if Andy has a fault, it's over-optimism. This is hardly a unique trait in chess players, but he's often especially unrealistic in post-mortems. Never ready to concede defeat, he often succeeds when others have thrown in the towel. On the other hand, there are plenty of times when he is left scratching his head wondering where it all went wrong, when probably in truth it was never going right!

'Ballistic' Bob
Arguably one of the craziest chess players around, Bob has never heard of playing it safe. He knows what he wants and he doesn't let anything stand in his way. Rarely restrained when it comes to sacrificing material, it's a surprise when he isn't giving away pieces! Give him his dues though, whilst most of the time he goes down in a ball of flames, his games are also littered with some stunningly beautiful combinations. In the pursuit of success he is prepared to

throw in all bar the kitchen sink and in fact once or twice even that's gone in too!

Another string to Bob's bow is his prowess at blitz chess. This stems from the marathon sessions he has playing five-minute chess down the local pub with his best mate, Harry 'the Hacker'.

'Cautious' Carol

'Calm' and 'composed' would also aptly describe Carol who if possible likes to keep things under control. Though uncomfortable in messy positions, she certainly has a knack of limiting her opponent's counterplay. Occasionally criticised for the great number of draws she has in competition play, she is however most proud of the fact that she once went two years without losing a single game!

'Devious' Dave

Dave is predictably unpredictable as with him you can always expect the unexpected! Certainly one of the sneakiest players around, the cogs in his brain are always working overtime as he contrives to trick his opponents. Frequently successful, if there is a drawback to his style it's that he does occasionally employ so much subtlety that in the cold light of day some of his plans just look too ridiculous!

'Steady' Eddy

Known as Ed to his friends, this is a guy that you can rely on, an honest citizen who never strays from the straight and narrow. Dependable in life and a solid chess player, his style over the board isn't exactly boring, although it's true that he generally adopts a no-thrills approach. There is a killer instinct there somewhere, but too often it seems that there is a line that he is not prepared to cross in order to achieve success. Just like Carol he rarely blunders and is unlikely to take unnecessary risks.

Help!

You've met the players and now this is where you come into play. Whose plan best fits the bill for each different situation? You decide and score points for correct answers. You'll find those in the back of the book, but take note. Carol was a late replacement for Chad 'the cheater'! No peeking from you either!

Before you move on, a few words of advice. Do not automatically assume that you can eliminate options simply through the wording. Occasionally there are some duff suggestions from our panel, but more frequently there is more than one reasonable suggestion. Eddy rarely makes mistakes and may suggest a very sensible approach. However, if there was a more ambitious continuation that was victorious in a real-life encounter then that will be rewarded. True, there is the argument that plans are often down to taste and even an individual's style. That's tough! I have handpicked these examples from top-level play and if the plans worked for them, then they work for me! However, I'd hate to be considered heartless, so I have awarded some points for plausible (but in my view, inferior!) suggestions.

Regarding my explanations in the answers (where the maximum point taker is in bold), I don't scrutinise every suggestion. I'd get bored constantly explaining why, for example, Dave is being too elaborate. It should be assumed that if I don't mention a nominated plan, then I'm not too enthused by it!

The tests are not related by themes or anything else. In the Solutions Overview at the end I have suggested a rough marking scheme, but there is no guarantee that you will get progressively higher scores. I hope that you will have fun working through the tests and by the end you should have improved your game from a strategy point of view. At the very least your eyes should have been opened to all sorts of new possibilities (though not all of them are recommended!).

Just one more thing: these tests aren't easy. Good luck!

Chris Ward,
London,
September 2000

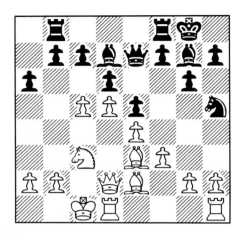

Position after 14...♛e7

White to move

There is no disputing that White has a space advantage here, but who has the best plan for how he should continue?

Andy

Andy wants to make much of his space advantage on the queenside. He believes that the c-file is 'where it's at' for his rooks, but would prefer not to open it until he is good and ready. He is radically advocating 15 b4, and obviously doesn't seem to mind exposing his king. Indeed he would expect the response 15...a5 when he then considers 16 cxd6 cxd6 17 b5 to be favourable as Black has weakened the b6-square with no real prospects of planting a knight on c5.

Bob

Bob has no hesitation in suggesting 15 g4. Usually he has no qualms in offloading a mere pawn, but here he accepts that c5xd6 may as well follow (no point giving away a pawn for absolutely nothing) before naturally continuing with h2-h4-h5. As far as Bob is concerned, it's only a matter of time before Black gets 'bashed' down the h-file, whereas with White not having moved any of the pawns around his own king, a similar pawn attack by Black would achieve little.

Carol

Carol would trade pawns immediately on d6. If Black recaptures with the queen then she likes 16 ♔b1 with her rooks naturally flooding to the c-file to pressurise the c7-pawn. Upon 15...cxd6 then ♔b1 and ♖c1 may follow later but particularly she favours 16 ♗h6. She has seen how often these black King's Indian bishops enter the game to devastating effect and this would remove such a possibility whilst offering kingside attacking options as well.

Dave

Dave likes the look of 15 c6. He regards the outside passed pawn that is created for the endgame after 15...bxc6 16 ♗xa6 as a real bonus. However, he acknowledges that we are far from an ending and sees this plan as a great way to obtain the d5-square for his knight (not unlikely in the event of 15...bxc6 and then an eventual ...c6xd5).

Eddy

After 15 cxd6 cxd6 Eddy wants to play 16 g3. This keeps the black knight out of f4 and in a rare moment of ambition, he dreams of playing f3-f4 himself. He values his dark-squared bishop and so wouldn't play 16 f4 immediately, but the thought of an extra pawn in the centre certainly appeals to him.

☐ Andy	☐ Bob	☐ Carol	☐ Dave	☐ Eddy

Points: ....

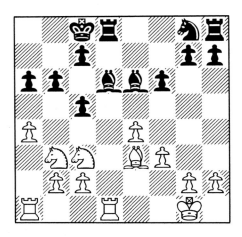

Position after 14...0-0-0

White to move

This position is typical of a Spanish (Ruy Lopez) Exchange. White has an 'effective' kingside majority to compensate him for his lost bishop pair. How should he attempt to make progress?

Andy

Andy has no hesitation whatsoever in suggesting an immediate king-side expansion starting with 15 g4 (with h2-h4-h5 next up). This pawn majority is where Andy sees his advantage and he thus wants to push these pawns immediately.

Bob

Bob isn't usually too enthralled by queenless middlegames like this, but can envisage some combinations on c5 (perhaps having jetti-soned the e-pawn as a deflection first). The key move for him though is 14 a5, letting a rook in and thus focusing the attention on

Black's a6-pawn.

Carol
Carol is quite happy to just double her rooks on the d-file and then tuck her king up to f2 where it's closer to the centre ready for the endgame. She believes that things will unfold in due course and with a mass exchange of rooks likely on the d-file, it's not unlikely that in the long run her kingside majority may prove decisive.

Dave
Dave believes that the b3-knight needs re-routing and sees the h5-square as a near perfect destination. It's a long journey but Dave sees ♘c1-e2-g3-h5 as a worthwhile investment.

Eddy
Eddy wants to buy a bit more space on the kingside and considers 14 h3 to be a good starting point. This keeps the g4-square firmly under White's control, making f3-f4 a perfectly satisfactory follow-up. Once the pawn is on f4, the e4-e5 break may not be long in coming and White may soon achieve his goal of obtaining a passed e-pawn.

☐ Andy   ☐ Bob   ☐ Carol   ☐ Dave   ☐ Eddy

Points: ....

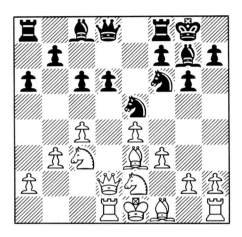

Position after 11 b3

Black to move

White has a very solid pawn structure and has piled up pressure on the natural target at d6. Black arguably has a better all-round development, but how should he react?

Andy

Despite the apparent bind on the key central post, Andy reckons that he can get away with the thematic 11...d5 break. Even if this loses a pawn, he believes that the centre should be opened up to his advantage. All of his pieces will spring to life and the white king will suffer in the centre.

Bob

Bob sees 11...♘fg4 as Black's answer. It's no surprise that Bob is prepared to sacrifice a piece and his justification here is that the white king is still in the centre and some time away from castling.

When the knight is captured White will then have to deal with his weak e-pawn and if he loses his dark-squared bishop, then he could soon feel full force of the King's Indian bishop.

Carol

11...♘e8 is the only move for Carol who doesn't like giving away pawns at the best of times. Sure, she acknowledges that it's a trifle passive, but sometimes you just have to bite the bullet.

Dave

Typically Dave has spotted a tactic in 11...♗h3. This of course cannot be taken because of the fork on f3 and in giving White something to think about on g2 and f3, Black has also connected his rooks.

Eddy

Though materialistic in nature, Eddy isn't too happy with Carol's idea and instead has decided that this is one of those positions where counter-attacking is the order of the day. He considered letting the d6-pawn go with the likes of 11...♗e6 and 11...♕a5, but in the end opted for the dynamic 11...b5, making sure that it's not all one-way traffic.

☐ Andy	☐ Bob	☐ Carol	☐ Dave	☐ Eddy

Points: ....

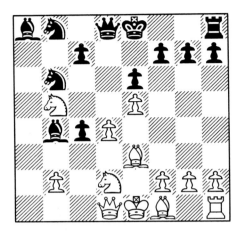

Position after 12...♝b4

White to move
White has the more solid pawn structure headed by a handy pairing in the centre. However, his piece co-ordination could be better, so how should he continue with his development?

Andy
Andy likes 13 ♖g1. This defends the g2-pawn, thus freeing the bishop, but also offers the idea of g2-g4. On g1 the rook will have escaped the pin by the bishop and can support a potential kingside pawn storm and thus attack.

Bob
Bob wants to introduce the rook via the immediate 13 h4. This places h4-h5-h6 on the menu and prepares ♖h3-g3. Bob doesn't like beating about the bush!

Carol

Carol favours 13 f3. As an alternative to castling she wants to put her king on f2 and her move also blocks out the a8-bishop. With that achieved she looks forward to being able to pick off the c4-pawn at her leisure.

Dave

Dave likes the multi-purpose move 13 ♕g4. On this square the queen defends both g2 and d4, but there is also another point to it. In hitting g7, Dave considers that he has serious attacking chances. Should Black castle kingside then White's dark-squared bishop will help with an offensive against the black king.

Eddy

Eddy has decided that he really wants to castle kingside as quickly as possible and has thus opted for 13 ♗e2. If Black captures on g2 then 14 ♖g1 gains the g7-pawn in return and when the white king is nice and safe he can then set about rounding up the c4-pawn.

☐ Andy   ☐ Bob   ☐ Carol   ☐ Dave   ☐ Eddy

Points: ....

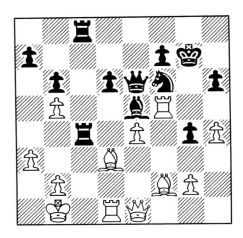

Position after 30 ♕e1

Black to move

Black appears to have built up quite an initiative on the queenside, but should he set about making that decisive breakthrough or is more prudence required?

Andy

Andy thought that he had found a win with 30...♖c2 but acknowledges that he sometimes gets carried away! In fact, he struggles to remember the win after 31 ♗xc2 but he is going to stick with this amazing move anyhow.

Bob

Bob thinks that this position is just his cup of tea. Tactically he feels that 30...♞xe4 will probably work, but he favours an attempt to prise open the white king. Even he is not ready for 30...♗xb2, but it's his belief that 30...♖a4 or 30...♖c3, both intending

31...♖xa3, are practically game, set and match.

Carol
Carol believes that it's better to be safe than sorry! She particularly likes the c-file domination that Black has achieved and seeks to preserve this with 30...♖4c7. This would also allow the black queen the chance to visit the b3-square.

Dave
Dave is happy to leave the attacked rook where it is and believes that despite so many active pieces at his disposal, the nail in White's coffin will be the black b-pawn. Indeed after 30...a6 his view is that ...b6-b5-b4 will soon follow, opening up the white king like a can of worms.

Eddy
Eddy is happy to make a rare positional exchange sacrifice and will thus leave the rook on c4. In order to obtain global domination (of the board!) he wants to tighten things up on the kingside with 30...h5. Then with everything safe on that side of the board he will set about infiltrating the white queenside with his own queen.

☐ Andy	☐ Bob	☐ Carol	☐ Dave	☐ Eddy

Points: ....

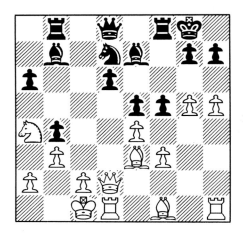

Position after 17...f5

White to move

Black has just struck out at the white centre with ...f7-f5 and White has a critical decision to make. Which one of our panel's plans appeals to you?

Andy

Andy reckons that after 19 &c4+ &h8, 20 h6 is the key move as 20...g6 21 f4 will soon fatally expose Black along the a1-h8 diagonal.

Bob

Bob has no hesitation in suggesting 18 &c4+ &h8 19 g6. He feels that Black will be positionally busted after 19...f4, but worse off still after 19...h6 20 &xh6 fxe4 21 &dg1 intending &xg7.

Carol

18 gxf6(e.p.) followed by 19 &e2 should leave White with a small

plus according to Carol and she is happy with that.

Dave
Dave wants to lure Black into taking the exchange with 18 exf5 ♗xf3 as then 19 ♗c4+ ♔h8 20 h6 is potentially a killer.

Eddy
Eddy likes 18 ♗c4+ ♔h8 19 ♗d5. This keeps things pretty much under control and specifically has in mind the long-term aim of securing the outpost on d5 for the white knight.

☐ Andy	☐ Bob	☐ Carol	☐ Dave	☐ Eddy

Points: ....

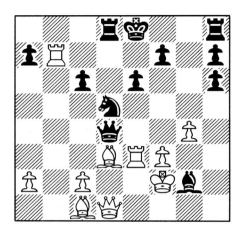

Position after 20...gxh6

White to move

In this rather wild position can anyone see a promising continuation for White?

Andy

Andy thinks that he has dreamt up a beautiful combination with 21 ♗g6. Indeed already picturing himself on the podium, in the only line that matters to him, 21...♕xd1, he's already found a glorious mate!

Bob

Bob disdainfully dismissed this position as trivially winning with 21 ♖xe6+ fxe6 22 ♗g6+ netting the black queen.

Carol

Carol claims that there is no chance of her getting into a position like this in the first place anyhow, and reluctantly offers 21 ♕e2. She will lose the exchange on e3, but expects to win the bishop on g2.

Dave

Dave has opted for the deceptively mundane 21 ♔xg2 in view of 21...♘xe3+ 22 ♗xe3 ♕xe3 23 ♕a1 when he expects the white queen to enter the black position to devastating effect.

Eddy

Eddy fancies the retreat 21 ♖b3. Black cannot castle anyhow in view of 22 ♗xh7+ and he feels that the rook can provide invaluable support along the 3rd rank.

☐ Andy	☐ Bob	☐ Carol	☐ Dave	☐ Eddy

Points: ....

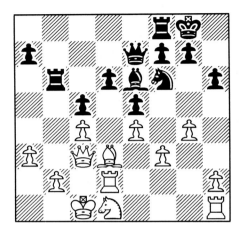

Position after 18 ♗d3

Black to move
Who has the best plan for improving Black's position?

Andy
Feeling that White is always going to be sufficiently protected on the queenside, Andy wants to seek action on the kingside beginning with 18...h5.

Bob
Of course ideally Bob would like employ ...♗xg4, but he suspects that this is unlikely to pan out. Instead he wants to blast open the position. The b-file was useful, but he wants the f-file and so is looking to arrange the pawn break ...f7-f5 somehow.

Carol
Never particularly radical, Carol is advocating a controlled trebling

of her major pieces on the b-file. Then she would like to improve the position of her knight with a manoeuvre to d4 a very realistic possibility.

Dave

Dave is thinking along the same lines as Andy but bearing in mind the presence of a 'bad' white light-squared bishop, he would like to secure complete domination on the dark squares first. Hence the surprising 18...g5 is his surprise choice to kick off the proceedings.

Eddy

Eddy wants to focus his attention on White's f3-pawn and has the likes of ...♘h7-g5 and ...♕f6 in mind. And that's just the short term! Then he wants ...♕f4 and a manoeuvre of his king's rook to f6.

□ Andy   □ Bob   □ Carol   □ Dave   □ Eddy

Points: ....

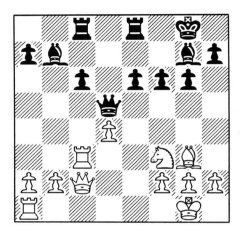

Position after 19 ♖c3

Black to move

Black has the advantage of the two bishops, but how should he best put this to use?

Andy

In a rather bizarre concept, Andy wants to advance both rooks' pawns. His idea is that ...a7-a5 will hold White up on the queenside whilst he can utilise ...h7-h5 in conjunction with ...g6-g5 to make headway on the kingside.

Bob

Blasting the position open with the immediate 19...e5 is the order of the day for Bob who wants to see his bishops getting in on the act sooner rather than later.

Carol

Carol believes that White will make it very difficult for Black to improve his (now her!) position and so suggests not making any further concessions. By sitting back and effectively not changing anything, Black can wait for White to overstretch.

Dave

Dave's idea is 19...f5, conceding an outpost on e5, but with the intention of preserving the bishop pair (in the event of 20 ♗e5) with 20...♗h6. His light-squared bishop may have to defend, but at least his dark-squared bishop will see some action.

Eddy

Eddy sees his c-pawn as his main weakness and so suggests a plan involving trading it off. He likes 19...♗f8 (intending ...c6-c5) and is certainly prepared to capture on a2 if White attempts to halt his master plan with 20 ♖c1.

☐ Andy	☐ Bob	☐ Carol	☐ Dave	☐ Eddy

Points: ....

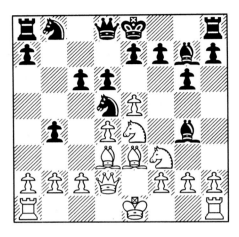

Position after 9...♘d5

White to move
White must be careful not to allow his central expansion campaign to backfire. How should he take it from here?

Andy
According to Andy the priority is to budge the d5-knight and he sees 10 c4 as the best way to do this. Even if Black captures en passant, 11 bxc3 will ensure that c3-c4 comes again soon!

Bob
10 0-0-0 is Bob's choice. He revels in positions of opposite-side castling and will be quick to launch a kingside offensive.

Carol
Carol believes that White has already got a little carried away, but that it's not too late to repair the damage. After 10 exd6 exd6, the

'swallowing the pride' 11 ♗e2 will leave White ready to castle king-side with little fear of reprisal.

Dave
Dave wants to save the tempo of 0-0-0 by going straight for it with 10 ♗h6. In order to prevent an immediate infiltration of the white queen, Black is obliged to castle kingside but then 11 h4 will be sur-prisingly dangerous despite White's apparent looseness in the cen-tre and the availability of ...♗xf3.

Eddy
Eddy doesn't really want to lose his dark-squared bishop to a knight, but he also wants to keep his centre intact. Weighing up the pros and cons he has arrived at 10 ♗f4, when he hopes that the mainte-nance of the e5-pawn will compensate for any problems elsewhere.

Now turn to page 108 for the solutions to Test One.

☐ Andy	☐ Bob	☐ Carol	☐ Dave	☐ Eddy
Points:				

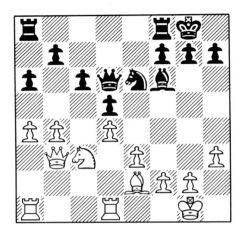

Position after 16 a4

Black to move
White intends a typical minority attack on the queenside. What is Black's best method of defence?

Andy
Attack! Black should launch a pawn storm against the white king. Starting with 16...g5, Andy intends ...♚g7, ...♖h8 and ...h7-h5 when Bob's your uncle! Well, actually he isn't, but once the black pawns come in direct confrontation with those surrounding the white king, his flimsy defence will be shown up for what it really is.

Bob
Bob likes Andy's attitude but believes that his idea is too long in getting to the point. 16...♘g5 is first up for him with a likely sacrifice on h3 to follow after ...♛d7.

Carol

Carol is not unduly worried by White's impending b4-b5 break and with the simple 16...♖fe8 (placing a rook on a half-open file) expects to be able to defend the weakness on c6 when it eventually arrives (obviously she won't capture on b5 as that would leave her with isolated d- and b-pawns).

Dave

Certainly not relishing the prospect of one-way traffic, Dave wants to give White something to think about. He believes that he must concentrate his efforts on the kingside and sees 16...♗d8 (intending 17...♗c7) as a good way of exploiting the h2-h3 'concession' that White has made. Indeed once White is forced into g2-g3 too, then ...♘g5 will offer serious sacrificial possibilities.

Eddy

Eddy doesn't like defending these sort of positions but if there is one thing that he has learnt about them, it's not to just sit back. Specifically 16...b5 is an idea that he has seen before (i.e. only after White has played b2-b4) when the black knight has the outpost on c4 to aim for. Once lodged there White will find it extremely difficult to generate play against the backward c6-pawn.

☐ Andy	☐ Bob	☐ Carol	☐ Dave	☐ Eddy
Points:				

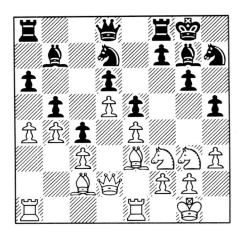

Position after 21...♖f8

White to move
In this Closed Spanish (Ruy Lopez) position, can you suggest a constructive plan for White?

Andy
Andy likes the idea of retreating the f3-knight to h2 and then 'blasting through' with the pawn break f2-f4. If Black allows this pawn to advance to f5 then he could soon be squashed, but if he trades pawns on f4 then his d6-pawn will be a target and Andy believes he may suffer down the f-file.

Bob
It's business as usual for Bob with 22 ♗h6. The black king will be his prey although he accepts that checkmate will not be on the cards for some time. Nevertheless, with the white rook available to swing into an attack via e3, he is optimistic.

Carol

Carol's choice is to seal things off on the queenside with 22 a5. This deprives a black knight of the b6-square and with ♖ad1 up next Carol hopes to limit Black's play in the centre. With all things considered Carol is expecting a draw, but she'll certainly be ready should Black try for more.

Dave

Dave has an amazing idea. He wants to treble major pieces on the a-file to take advantage of the tension over there (i.e. the situation revolving around the a4 and b5-pawns). This may facilitate an invasion of Black's position when he is ready to trade pawns and he also has his eye on winning the b5-pawn too. To accomplish this he has an extravagant idea of manoeuvring a knight to b1 from where it can go to a3 once the queens and rooks have been eliminated.

Eddy

Eddy favours simple chess here: 22 ♖eb1 followed by ♕d1(or e1). Then a trade of pawns on b5 and rook swaps along the a-file. No-thrills chess it's true, but Eddy still anticipates retaining a slight advantage.

☐ Andy	☐ Bob	☐ Carol	☐ Dave	☐ Eddy

Points: ....

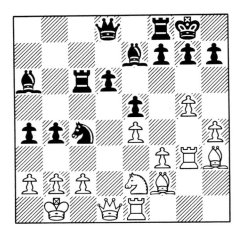

Position after 23 ♕d1

Black to move
Compared to Black's pieces, the white ones look awkwardly placed. How should the second player set about exploiting this?

Andy
Andy feels that his f8-rook is the only one not pulling its weight. Hence he has come up with 23...f6, which should result in it being activated to the detriment of White's f3-pawn.

Bob
It's no surprise that Bob is all for 23...♘a3+. After the forced 24 bxa3 the white king will be fatally exposed by simply 24...bxa3 (one obvious threat being 24...♕b8+-b2 mate).

Carol
Carol is a little worried by White's attacking possibilities and would

like to flick in 23...g6 before attempting to make headway against the white king.

Dave
Dave likes 23...a3 as it puts a question to White for which he believes there is no answer. 24 b3 is forced when all Black needs to do is set about manoeuvring his queen down to b2.

Eddy
Eddy's first thought was to vacate the queen (say to a5) in order to connect the rooks. However, he then came up with 23...d5. This is not a sacrifice in view of ...♖d6, but he sees the d-file as the only extra ingredient required to win the game.

☐ Andy	☐ Bob	☐ Carol	☐ Dave	☐ Eddy

Points: ....

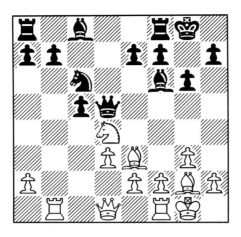

Position after 12 ♘d4

Black to move
Black has previously won a pawn and in a murky position can consider grabbing on a2. Any suggestions?

Andy
Andy is all for 12...♕xa2. After 13 ♘xc6 bxc6 14 ♗xc6 he has 14...♗h3 and he feels that if White does ever trap his queen, he will have accumulated adequate material for it by that stage.

Bob
In a radical change from his usual style, Bob is prepared to offload his queen with 12...♕xg2+. This is a very important bishop and gaining the knight on d4 next his position will be ultra solid with an extra pawn to be pushed at his leisure.

Carol

Carol is happy retreating the queen back to d6. Although she knows that she will receive doubled c-pawns, a future ...♝d4 will help her to retain the c5-pawn.

Dave

Dave wants to slide the black queen over to the kingside. With 12...♛h5, the black queen remains defending the c5-pawn, attacks White's e2-pawn and facilitates ...♝h3.

Eddy

Eddy's opinion is the same as that of Carol's except that he prefers 12...♛d7 first instead of 12...♛d6.

☐ Andy	☐ Bob	☐ Carol	☐ Dave	☐ Eddy

Points: ....

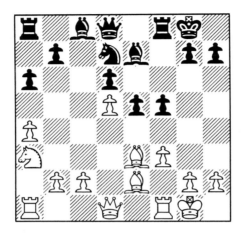

Position after 14 f3

Black to move

How should Black utilise his space advantage on the kingside?

Andy

According to Andy, by throwing still further pawns up the board. 14...g5 followed by 15...h5 and unless there is other business to attend to, 16...g4 would be next.

Bob

No sacrificing just yet, but Bob isn't afraid to make the positional concession of the e4-square with 14...f4. After the bishop retreats, Bob wants to launch a kingside attack with the likes of ...♛e8-h5 and ...♜f6-h6.

Carol

Carol is in favour of trading off the bishops with 14...♗g5. In exchanging off her bad bishop (for White's good one), she also hopes to be able to exploit the weak dark squares in the white camp.

Dave
Another intriguing idea from Dave. He wants to play 14...e4, but not with the intention of simply creating a passed pawn. No, he has it mind to meet 15 fxe4 with 15...♘e5. This is an excellent square for his knight and to boot he has freed up his light-squared bishop. He believes that this is worth a pawn.

Eddy
Eddy wants to make the defensive e7-bishop into more of a good King's Indian one. This entails 14...g6 with ...♗f6 and if necessary ....♗g7 to follow later.

☐ Andy	☐ Bob	☐ Carol	☐ Dave	☐ Eddy
Points:				

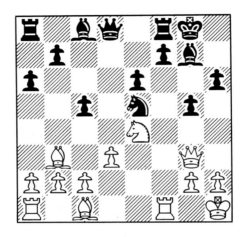

Position after 16...0-0

White to move

White has good piece play but has sacrificed a pawn in order to get this position. Is the time now right for something radical?

Andy

Yes, 17 ♘xg5 is Andy's choice. After 17...hxg5 18 ♗xg5, Black will be unable to deal with the double threat of 19 ♗h6 and 19 ♗f6.

Bob

Bob's preference is for 17 ♗xg5. After 17...hxg5 18 ♘xg5 (threatening ♕h4-h7) Bob cannot guarantee a win but believes that he is not worse and that he can capitalise on any inaccurate black defence.

Carol

No, Carol suggests re-establishing material equality with 17 ♘xc5.

There's not much in it, but she suspects that White has a slight edge due to the holes around the black king.

Dave

Dave doesn't believe that anything too radical is required. He wants to worm his way into the black king position with 17 h4.

Eddy

The problem with 17 ♘xc5 according to Eddy is that it enables Black to develop his queenside bishop more than satisfactorily with 17...b6 (and ...♗b7). Eddy favours a slow build-up instead. 17 ♗d2 comes first with a doubling of the rooks on the f-file and (if allowed) ♘f6+ to follow.

☐ Andy   ☐ Bob   ☐ Carol   ☐ Dave   ☐ Eddy

Points: ....

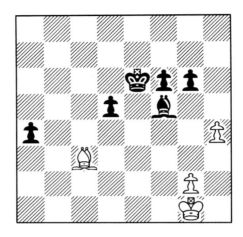

Position after 47 ♔g1

Black to move

Opposite-coloured bishop endgames are often very drawish. Black has two extra pawns here but is there a suitable plan to realise this material advantage?

Andy

Andy believes that he can afford to offload his bishop with 47...♗h3. He suggests that this amazing piece sacrifice allows him quick access to offer support to his passed pawns.

Bob

Often disinterested in endgames, Bob wants to go straight for glory with 47...d4. In offloading the d-pawn he can buy himself the tempi required to ensure winning White's bishop for his a-pawn.

Carol
Carol wants to play 47...&e4 as it hits the g2-pawn. Then 48...f5 will follow (placing this pawn out of danger) with an infiltration of White's queenside by the black king (to aid the promotion of the a-pawn) as the icing on the cake.

Dave
Dave is in no hurry to advance his passed pawns and is more concerned with sorting out the situation on the kingside. He feels that this is best done with 47...g5. Once 1 vs. 1 is obtained on the g-file, Black can then set about sewing things up elsewhere.

Eddy
Eddy feels that it's vital that the a-pawn negotiates the a3-square immediately before White can set up a dark-squared blockade. After 47...a3, 48...a2 will follow with the black king then seeking entry even via a4 if necessary. Should the white king attempt to deny its enemy number access then Eddy is sure that there will be some ducking and diving available.

□ Andy	□ Bob	□ Carol	□ Dave	□ Eddy
Points:				

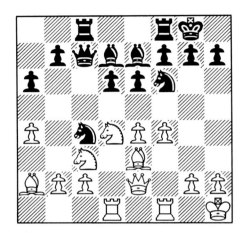

Position after 14...♘c4

White to move

What approach should White adopt in this game?

Andy

Andy concedes that he must chop on c4 with the bishop to remove the annoying black knight. However, after 15...♕xc4 he can then avoid a trade of queens with 16 ♖d3. A rook along the 3rd rank will provide a good springboard for an eventual attack against the black king.

Bob

The knight doesn't bother Bob. Ignoring the attacks on b2 and e3 he prefers to preserve his light-squared bishop and get on with things via a familiar theme. The confident Bob likes 15 ♖f3 and on 15...♘xb2, 16 ♖g3. He is of the view that Black's extra pieces won't do him much good when he is mated on g7!

Carol

The Open Sicilian isn't Carol's favourite type of position, but going with general principles she suggests preserving the bishop pair with 15 ♗c1. She then rather nervously suggests a follow up of g2-g4-g5 with f4-f5, hoping to secure an outpost on d5.

Dave

Dave likes the immediate 15 f5 as tactics on e6 will favour him after 15...♘xb2. Alternatively 15...e5 will concede an important outpost on d5.

Eddy

15 ♗xc4 ♕xc4 16 ♕d3 is Eddy's suggestion, and he assesses the resulting position as equal. He has adopted a realistic approach. There are many times when crazy Open Sicilians result in fantastic successful attacking encounters. On the other hand there are plenty of glorious failures too!

☐ Andy	☐ Bob	☐ Carol	☐ Dave	☐ Eddy

Points: ....

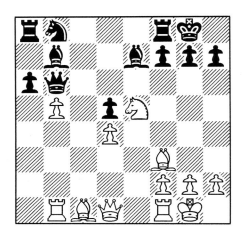

Position after 16...♛b6

White to move

Black's d5-pawn is obviously a hindrance to him, but how should White set about capitalising on this?

Andy

In general Andy feels that White should dedicate all of his resources to trying to win this pawn. That is a major plan in itself, but one that he feels is likely to be successful.

Bob

Bob believes that the key to winning this game ultimately lies with his f-pawn. First for him would come 17 ♗h5. This hits a target point f7 and makes way a potential f2-f4-f5-f6. Should Black respond with 17...g6 then this just adds to the force that will be felt by Black when f2-f4-f5 arrives.

Carol

Carol favours the immediate 17 ♛d3 which, whilst offering support to the b5-pawn, has a nice central feel to it. The bishop can come out next to f4 whilst Black will find it difficult to complete his development.

Dave

Dave likes the look of 17 ♖e1 because it offers discovered attack possibilities on the e7-bishop. If Black doesn't capture on b5, then 18 ♛d3 should follow with White essentially having control over the whole board.

Eddy

Eddy believes that White's light-squared bishop has no further use on its current diagonal. By retreating it to e2 he can protect his b5-pawn and then by nudging it up to d3 he can generate serious attacking chances against the enemy king.

☐ Andy　　☐ Bob　　☐ Carol　　☐ Dave　　☐ Eddy

Points:　...............

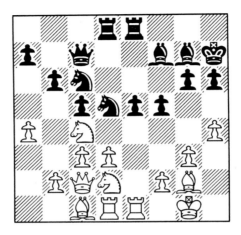

Position after 21 h4

Black to move
Black didn't move first, but he seems to have built up a nice space advantage! How can he try to convert this into something even more substantial?

Andy
Andy is advocating the positional piece sacrifice 21...♘db4. He will pick up the d3-pawn and then retain the embedded knight by supporting it with ...e5-e4 and perhaps even ...c5-c4.

Bob
No messing around by Bob. He wants to ram his f-pawn into White's position and there is no time like the present! 21...f4 will shortly be followed by ...g6-g5-g4 and ...f4-f3.

Carol

Carol is happy that White can't break free of his shackles with d3-d4, but is worried about the counterplay that may be sought through b2-b4 or a4-a5. On this front she feels that she can kill two birds with one stone; that stone being 21...a5. Ultimately she believes that she can win by picking off White's d3-pawn.

Dave

Dave reckons that the key to winning this position is getting in ...e5-e4. This will open up the diagonal for the g7-bishop and present Black with the e5-square. He feels that the latter square could be used to devastating effect by a black knight.

Eddy

Eddy wants to double his rooks on the e-file and then play ...h6-h5.

Now turn to page 115 for the solutions to Test Two.

Now turn to page 115 for the solutions to Test Two.

☐ Andy   ☐ Bob   ☐ Carol   ☐ Dave   ☐ Eddy

Points: ....

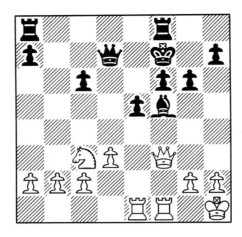

Position after 18...♔f7

White to move
How should White handle this position?

Andy
The black king is clearly heading for safety on g7 or g8. Andy therefore is suggesting 'softening up' Black's kingside with 19 h4-h5.

Bob
There is simply no way that Bob would be able to refrain from 19 g4. It's hardly a sacrifice as White will pick up Black's f- and e-pawns as well as causing grief to the black king with his queen and rooks.

Carol
With care! Carol believes that there is danger for White if he over-

overstretches and instead advises him to effectively do nothing. By holding his ground he should be able to draw, with winning chances only if Black gets too fruity.

Dave

Dave goes with Bob's 19 g4 but after 19...♗xg4 20 ♕xf6+ ♔g8 wants to play 21 ♕g5 instead of 21 ♕xe5. His presumption is that on g5 the queen is safe from hassle and the road is clear for ♘e4-f6+.

Eddy

Eddy also likes the idea of playing g2-g4 in order to get at Black's f-pawn and at the very least dissuade a future ...f6-f5. However, his more restrained view is that it must be preceded by the more cautious 19 h3.

□ Andy   □ Bob   □ Carol   □ Dave   □ Eddy

Points: ....

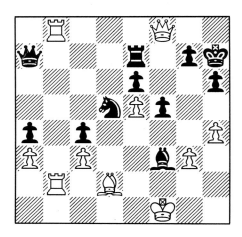

Position after 45 ♖1b2

Black to move
Despite the dangerous-looking white queen and rook on Black's back rank, his active pieces provide good compensation for the exchange. How can he improve his position though?

Andy
45...f4 is the key move for Andy who wants to get at the white king along the f-file. He feels that his rook is the one piece that he could do with improving and so fancies meeting the anticipated 46 gxf4 with 46...♖f7.

Bob
It's 45...♘e3+ for Bob as after 46 ♗xe3 ♕xe3, Black can happily offer his rook for the ultimate cause of giving checkmate. White has no perpetual check whilst the queen and bishop combination prove too deadly.

Carol

Carol thinks that this position is a virtual stalemate. Neither side can improve significantly without fear of extreme reprisal. The superb d5-knight will only hop into e3 if the b2-rook leaves its current post on the second rank. Meanwhile, the black queen can just alternate squares along its current diagonal if it comes under attack.

Dave

With a sneaky mating net up his sleeve, Dave likes the look of 45...♗g4. His idea is 46...♗h3+ with ...♕g1 to follow. Once this is achieved mate is inevitable whilst his own king, covered by his rook, is in no danger whatsoever.

Eddy

Eddy was tempted to go with Carol's view, but then decided that there is a piece that he can introduce to the action. His king! Yes, he believes that it's safe to dabble in the likes of 45...♔g6-h5-g4 if allowed.

☐ Andy   ☐ Bob   ☐ Carol   ☐ Dave   ☐ Eddy

Points: ....

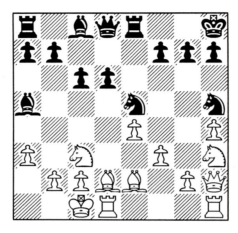

Position after 14 ♗e2

Black to move
A position with plenty of plans available to Black. Which of the ones put forward looks the most promising?

Andy
Andy believes that White is itching to get on with his wing play. The best reaction then is to strike out in the centre and 14...d5 is his solution. With the centre opened up he expects White's kingside pieces to be caught napping 'out on a limb'.

Bob
Bob's view is that if White wants a war, he's sure going to get one! With 14...b5, Black will set the ball rolling. He expects the likes of g2-g4 and h4-h5, but as White has detrimentally moved a pawn around his own king already (a3) a plan of ...a7-a5 (after dropping the bishop back to b6 or c7) and then ...b5-b4 will hit home first.

Carol

Carol wants to limit White's possibilities and that includes depriving the opponent of the g5-square. Before she begins play in the centre (she feels that a queenside attack will be too slow), a precautionary 14...h6 is her nomination.

Dave

Dave knows that it's usually wrong to just concede bishops for knights. However, here he believes that 14...♗xh3 hits the mark. 15 gxh3 would drop the h4-pawn whilst 15 ♕xh3 walks into 15...♗xc3. As 16 bxc3 would then be forced (not 16 ♗xc3 ♘f4), White would suffer for his wrecked pawn structure.

Eddy

Simple development is what is required here. Nothing flashy, just 14...♗e6 (which eyes up the c4-square) followed by a careful introduction for the major pieces.

☐ Andy	☐ Bob	☐ Carol	☐ Dave	☐ Eddy

Points: ....

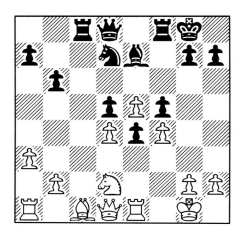

Position after 18 f4

Black to move

White has a bad bishop and his opponent has a good bishop. Can you suggest where the second player should focus his attention?

Andy

On the kingside according to Andy. He wants more light squares in important areas. A plan of 18...g6 followed by ...h5-h4-h3 should lead to a big thorn in White's position.

Bob

'No point in hanging around,' says Bob (what a surprise!) who favours the immediate 18...g5. The g-file will prove critical in a swift and merciless destruction of the white king (or at the very least he should win a pawn or two!).

Carol

Carol is happy with her position and wants to relocate her knight on c6 in order to pressurise White's d4-pawn. 18...♞b8 is first, but ...♝c4 may follow if the white knight moves from d2.

Dave

Dave has a bit more subtlety in mind. He likes the idea of exploiting White's light-squared holes on the queenside and so wants to probe with 18...b5 followed by ...a7-a5-a4.

Eddy

Eddy has a similar idea to Carol, but he prefers 18...♜e8 with the intention of ...♞f8-e6.

☐ Andy	☐ Bob	☐ Carol	☐ Dave	☐ Eddy
Points:				

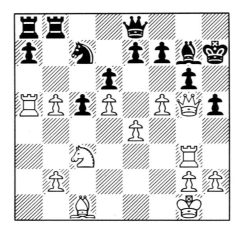

Position after 23...♔h7

White to move

White has built up a strong initiative on the kingside, but Black is ready to break through on the queenside. Does White need to act quickly?

Andy

Andy believes that there is time for a 24 ♘e2-f4 manoeuvre. Surely then there will be no way for Black to withstand the pressure created on h5 and g6.

Bob

Bob is hardly one to panic, but he's certainly never backward in coming forward! The attacked b-pawn is no problem to him. He likes the idea of 24 ♖h3 intending to meet 24...♘xb5 by 25 ♘xb5 ♖xb5 26 ♖aa3 with a crushing sacrifice on h5 imminent.

Carol
Because she is attacking e7 with her queen, Carol believes that she is indirectly protecting the b5-pawn. She is however a little worried about the back rank and is advocating 24 h3 to prevent any future disasters in that area.

Dave
Dave believes that now is the time for action. He is slightly surprised that Bob has not gone for 24 e5 dxe5 25 d6 exd6 26 ♞e4 as he likes the look of this. The knight would be extremely powerful there where it both attacks Black's d-pawn and threatens ♞f6+.

Eddy
Eddy is quite calm about the whole situation. He can see no obvious breakthrough just yet, but feeling under no great pressure (thanks to his queen hitting e7), is happy to continue building up with 24 ♗d2.

☐ Andy	☐ Bob	☐ Carol	☐ Dave	☐ Eddy
Points:				

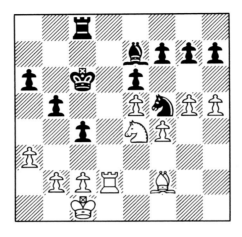

Position after 32 ♖d2

Black to move
Black has a well placed knight and the better bishop. How can he try
to win this endgame?

Andy
According to Andy he must expand on the queenside. 32...a5 and
soon ...b5-b4 is what he has in mind when he will later be able to
choose between the promising options ...b4-b3 and ...c4-c3.

Bob
I had to wake up Bob a couple of times to get his final decision,
which was the rather anti-positional looking 32...b4. His logic is that
after 33 axb4 ♗xb4 he is likely to be able to get in the critical
...c4-c3.

Carol

Carol wants to cancel out White's edge on the d-file. By opposing rooks (32...♖d8) she feels that after the inevitable trade White will be powerless for her waltz through the centre in order to capture the over-extended kingside pawns.

Dave

Dave likes 32...g6. This is played under the premise of fixing a pawn on the opposite-coloured square to his remaining bishop, but his really devious ploy is to obtain the h-file for his rook.

Eddy

Eddy wants to utilise his own rook to help hassle the enemy kingside pawns. With 32...♖h8 he intends 33...h6. This immediately pressurises the h5-pawn and if White's rook is called into action over there, the likes of ...♔d5 will become available.

☐ Andy   ☐ Bob   ☐ Carol   ☐ Dave   ☐ Eddy

Points: ....

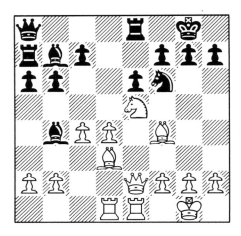

Position after 15...♗b4

White to move

Black's a7-rook looks ridiculously placed, but his queen and bishop are hitting g2. More to the point White's rook is en prise to the dark-squared bishop. How should White deal with these threats?

Andy

Andy feels that he can sacrifice the exchange, but it's Black's light-squared bishop that he wants. After 16 ♖f1 ♗xg2 he likes f2-f3 when Black will win material but will suffer the consequences of the now massive hole on c6. Added to this White will be able to arrange a nifty attack along the g-file.

Bob

Bob is also not too bothered about his e1-rook as he considers Black's dark-squared bishop to be a good defender. He sets his sights on the f6-knight and his plan is to kill two birds with one stone via 16 g4 (intending g4-g5 and good attacking chances on h7).

Carol

Carol thinks that 16 ♗d2 is forced. After 16...♗xd2 17 ♖xd2, Black will be unable to capture on g2 because 18 f3, trapping the bishop, and otherwise White just has a comfortable plus.

Dave

Effectively Dave wants to block out all of Black's queenside pieces with 16 d5. Sure this is an exchange sacrifice, but he feels that he will then have a material advantage where things really count on the kingside.

Eddy

Eddy became uncharacteristically adventurous here. He went along with Carol's 16 ♗d2, but after 16...♗xd2 fancied dabbling with 17 ♕xd2. His idea is to meet 17...♗xg2 with 18 ♕g5 gaining a tempo on Black's bishop. The queen is on an excellent post on g5 and White can instigate a serious offensive with ♖e3-g3.

☐ Andy   ☐ Bob   ☐ Carol   ☐ Dave   ☐ Eddy

Points: ....

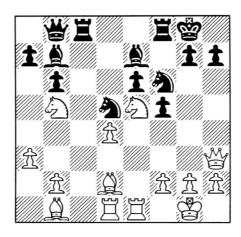

Position after 20...♛b8

White to move

As is consistent with an Isolated Queen's Pawn (IQP) position,
White had previously attacked the h7-square. This was foiled by
...f7-f5. What should he try now?

Andy

Having provoked weaknesses in Black's kingside, Andy believes that
now the time has come to start work on the queenside. Starting
with 21 a4, a plan of a4-a5xb6 should saddle Black with the necessary extra weakness required before White can think in terms of
gaining the full point.

Bob

Bob's view is that Black has only temporarily held up the proceedings on the kingside. Now is the time for White to blast through
and he should not waste any time in playing 21 f3. Sure, this has the

benefit of blocking off the b7-g2 diagonal, but the real idea behind it is of course 22 g4.

Carol
Carol wants to secure the outpost on e5 with 21 f4. Then having already fulfilled its task (of provoking ...f7-f5) she wants to bring her queen back to a more central role on d3 before doubling her rooks on the c-file.

Dave
Dave's plan, which takes up a few moves, includes manoeuvring his light-squared bishop to f3 and then following ♗g5 with ♘d3-f4. These three minor pieces will then be on their optimum squares, making life hell for Black particularly regards his e6-pawn.

Eddy
Eddy's opinion of these IQP positions is that once Black blocks the b1-h7 diagonal with ...f7-f5, White should relocate his light-squared bishop to the a2-g8 diagonal. Ultimately then his aim is to focus his attention on Black's e6-pawn.

☐ Andy   ☐ Bob   ☐ Carol   ☐ Dave   ☐ Eddy

Points: ....

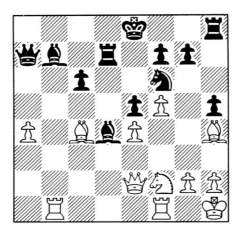

Position after 24...♛a7

White to move
Bearing in mind Black's errant h-pawn, his king is in a bit of a quandary. How might White seek to take advantage of this fact?

Andy
Whilst the h8-rook is out of play, Andy feels that White should concentrate on pushing his a-pawn. 25 ♛a2 is the best place to start with a4-a5-a6 following pretty much come what may.

Bob
Not for the first time the move g2-g4 has entered into Bob's mind! At a glance even he thought it was a ridiculous idea as it could possibly help activate both black rooks and provide the enemy light-squared bishop with options along the exposed b7-h1 diagonal. However, his justification is that Black's pieces remain uncoordinated whilst 25...♝xf2 (i.e. after 25 g4) does not win a pawn because 26

♗xf2 hits the black queen.

Carol
With Black being so tied up Carol feels that there is no need to panic. Her choice is to switch the bishop to c2 (via 25 ♗b3) where it defends both a4 and e4. Then her masterplan is to double rooks on the b-file.

Dave
Dave also believes that the a-pawn is the key to victory for White. With the queen where it is on e2 he 'knows' that Black can't castle. His star move is the exchange sacrifice 25 ♖a1. If Black takes it with his bishop then he will have lost his best piece whilst White would still finish with a rook behind an extremely dangerous passed pawn.

Eddy
Eddy has the f7-pawn in his sights. He likes 25 ♘h3 and once 26 ♘g5 has been played he suspects that some tactical delicacies will appear.

☐ Andy	☐ Bob	☐ Carol	☐ Dave	☐ Eddy

Points: ....

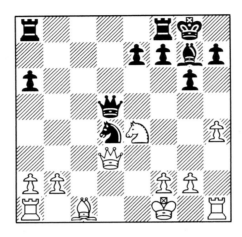

Position after 22 h4

Black to move
White's position seems to be in disarray. How might Black capitalise on this?

Andy
Andy feels nicely centralised already and considers that the best way to make progress here is to put the so often vital fianchettoed bishop to work. Although there are several good moves, most accurate for him is 22...a5 with ...a5-a4-a3 on the cards.

Bob
Bob remarks that White has a cheek attacking him with the likes of 22 h4 and wants to get his own offensive under way first with 22...f5. The intention naturally is to roll this f-pawn down the board and into the heart of the white position.

Carol

Simple chess is the attitude that Carol is adopting here. She favours 22...♖fd8 with 23...♖ac8 to follow, when she feels that White will ultimately have no defence to threats in the middle.

Dave

Dave has foreseen the potential problems that he may experience down the h-file with no doubt h4-h5 next on White's agenda. Hence he feels he should get in 22...h5 himself. Then he can play ...f7-f6 and ...e7-e5 with ...♔h7, facilitating a trade of his bad bishop with ...♗h6.

Eddy

According to Eddy, any chance of a white kingside attack should be dashed by trading the queens. For him 22...♕b5 hits the mark when his view is that he may be able to convert his endgame advantage.

Now turn to page 122 for the solutions to Test Three.

Now turn to page 122 for the solutions to Test Three.

☐ Andy	☐ Bob	☐ Carol	☐ Dave	☐ Eddy
Points:				

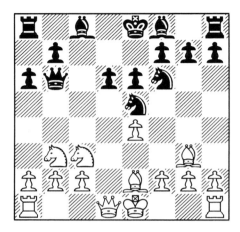

Position after 10 ♗g3

Black to move

There are a variety of ways for Black to develop his pieces, but is it the time for something a little different?

Andy

Yes, Andy likes 10...h5 with the intention of hassling the currently comfortable bishop on g3 with ...h5-h4. This should certainly dissuade White from the quick f2-f4 and e4-e5 that he may have had in mind.

Bob

With a lack of pieces in play at the moment, even Bob doesn't believe that this is the time for anything too radical. He is happy to continue with 10...♗d7 (and perhaps ...♗c6); he fancies castling queenside particularly if the white king goes short.

Carol

No, Carol can see no justification for anything other than the straightforward 10...♗e7 and almost certainly 11...0-0. If nothing critical happens, only then she will choose between ...♗d7 and ...♕c7, ...b7-b5 and ...♗b7.

Dave

On a completely different track, Dave fancies pressurising White's queenside. Specifically he is attracted to 10...a5, which threatens to budge the b3-knight with 11...a4. Should White opt to halt this pawn's progress with a2-a4 himself then he will have irreconcilably weakened the b4-square.

Eddy

Eddy is usually one for swift castling, but here he recognises the necessity to halt a steamroller of white pawns. For him an important move is 10...g5 as it binds the f4-square. His dark-squared bishop then has options and ...h7-h5-h4 may follow later.

□ Andy	□ Bob	□ Carol	□ Dave	□ Eddy

Points: ....

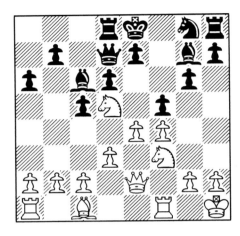

Position after 11...♖d8

White to move
Black has the advantage of the two bishops but is behind in development and has some undesirable holes. How might White set about exploiting his opponent's deficiencies?

Andy
Andy wants to lock out the g7-bishop and control the f6-square. He feels that the knight has done its job on d5 and so is advocating 12 ♘c3 with the intention of 13 e5. Black's knight will then be stuck and a timely e5-e6 could prove extremely awkward.

Bob
Bob wants to wade in with 12 ♘g5. He believes that Black will be put to the sword swiftly when ♘e6 arrives and once his other knight moves say to c4 via b6, e4xf5 will make this a distinct possibility.

Carol

Carol wants to build up her centre. With 12 c3 she will blunt the g7-bishop, but the main aim is to get in d3-d4. The e4-e5 advance is also likely to follow in the future with the situation of her currently attacked d5-knight likely to resolve itself soon.

Dave

Dave likes 12 a4. He has observed that this pawn cannot be captured in view of 13 ♘b6 and indeed the b6-square will be a fantastic permanent outpost once the intended a4-a5 is achieved. The position will practically play itself from there on in.

Eddy

Eddy wants to support his well placed central knight further with 12 c4. After 'binding' the d5-square, he will continue simply with the likes of ♗d2-c3 and ♖ae1. His opinion is that the black position will crack under the pressure.

☐ Andy	☐ Bob	☐ Carol	☐ Dave	☐ Eddy

Points: ....

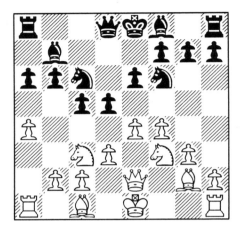

Position after 9 ♗g2

Black to move
From Black's point of view, what are your thoughts on this position?

Andy
Andy wants to grab some space advantage with the immediate 9...d4. Once the c3-knight budges he will logically aim to consider his queenside play with the likes of ...b6-b5 (and eventually ...c5-c4) but only after getting his king into safety with 10...♗e7 and 11...0-0.

Bob
Bob would rather have White's position as he would anticipate good attacking chances with what he considers to be an inevitable f4-f5 break. However, he suggests that Black can get the ball rolling first with 9...h5. He can attack along the h-file and his own king is only a stone's throw from castling queenside.

Carol

Carol wants to leave the tension in the centre and has decided that 9...♗e7 with 10...0-0 coming next is the most accurate continuation. Should White get fruity on the kingside then she has the option to open things up with ...d5xe4, but that aside she will seek some queenside expansion.

Dave

Though often accused of trying to be too clever, Dave has decided here that he can temporarily forgo the obvious development moves in favour of the sharp 9...♘d4. If things go to plan he may get an annoying ...♗b4+ instead of just ...♗e7.

Eddy

With a no-risk policy here, Eddy wants to trade pawns immediately on e4 to avoid what he considers to be a dangerous attack that could emerge if White gets in e4-e5, g3-g4, f4-f5 etc. With both kings likely to be heading for the kingside the latter is a scenario that he would rather avoid.

☐ Andy	☐ Bob	☐ Carol	☐ Dave	☐ Eddy
Points:				

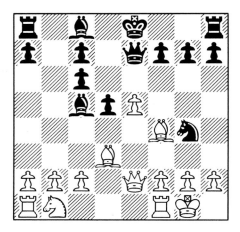

Position after 10 ♗f4

Black to move

It could be that Black's g4-knight is out on a limb. How should he
deal with this situation.

Andy

Andy thinks 10...f6 is what is required to buy time for the knight to
return to action. A trade a of queens after 11 exf6 will be fine by
him as the black king is nearer the centre and thus ready for the
ensuing endgame.

Bob

There is no doubt in Bob's mind that he should play 10...g5 and after
11 ♗g3 he must not allow the initiative to slip. Thus he should per-
severe with 11...h5. The threat is ...h5-h4 and the pressure on f2
should also help divert attention away from his knight.

Carol

Here Carol is opting for 10...h5. She doesn't believe that she has serious attacking chances but rather wants to provide the knight with a satisfactory retreat square. From h6 it will later be able to swing out to the promising f5-square.

Dave

Dave has come up with the amazing 10...♖g8. This outrageous continuation sees Black happy to jettison the h7-pawn to White's bishop (as then the rook will return to h8 where it will be on an attractive half-open file). Dave wouldn't expect White to capture on h7, but he would anticipate 11 h3. This is when his devious concept really becomes clear. After 11...♘h6 12 ♗xh6 gxh6 the rook ends on a handy half-open file anyhow!

Eddy

After much consideration (Eddy thinks that this is a difficult position) he has plumped for 10...♗e6. He will leave his king in the centre for as long as possible before deciding upon which side he should castle.

| ☐ Andy | ☐ Bob | ☐ Carol | ☐ Dave | ☐ Eddy |

Points: ....

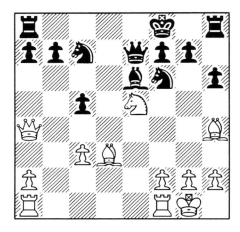

Position after 26...♔f8

White to move

White clearly has some compensation for his sacrificed pawn, but how is the best way for him to continue so as not to let Black off the hook?

Andy

Andy anticipates that Black will have to attempt to escape the pin of his f6-knight soon with ...g7-g5. Hence he is selecting 27 ♖ae1 so that his f-rook will provide the firepower behind a future f2-f4.

Bob

Guess what, Bob likes 27 g4. He wants to thrash Black with 28 g5 and he can see no point in hanging around!

Carol

Though uncomfortable about being a pawn down, Carol thinks that a simple doubling of rooks on the d-file (beginning with 27 ♖ad1) is a sensible enough plan. She believes that domination there will provide long-term pressure and she dreams of a time when ♘d7 may become available.

Dave

Dave likes the crafty 27 f3. His idea is 28 ♘g4 which pressurises f6. It's the black knight that he believes he should be singling out for attention and the subtle point behind 27 f3 is that if Black's light-squared bishop captures on g4, then f3xg4 would open up his rook on the f-file (still hitting f6!).

Eddy

Eddy toyed with the idea of 27 f4 as he feels that his f-pawn should have a part to play somewhere. However, eventually he decided that he should give priority to the centralisation of his rooks. He has given 27 ♖fe1 the nod with ♖ad1 to follow next.

☐ Andy	☐ Bob	☐ Carol	☐ Dave	☐ Eddy

Points: ....

Position after 69...♔g4

White to move
If White plays accurately is there any way that he can realistically expect to win this minimal material endgame?

Andy
Yes, according to Andy, but he can't afford to waste any time. He must dash back with his king (70 ♔c6 is the only move) when he will arrive just in time along with his rook to prevent Black from pro-moting.

Bob
'Not on your Nelly!' is Bob's view. Provided that Black doesn't play like a drain it's going to be a draw anyway, so White might as well whip off the pawn as soon as possible with his rook and stop wasting both player's time!

Carol

Carol is cautious, but she believes that she is never going to have to give up the rook for the pawn. However, despite agreeing with 70 ♔c6, unlike Andy she has calculated that Black will be forced to promote to a knight. With this minor piece trapped on the back rank her king and rook will win the day.

Dave

Dave has observed that Black intends to use his own king as a sort of battering ram to prevent the white monarch from participating in an active defence. He therefore believes that 70 ♖f6 is necessary to cut the king off when he has analysed the game out to a win for him.

Eddy

Eddy likes his endgame principles and with 70 ♖g6 he is going with one that has served him well on numerous occasions in the past: Rooks belong behind passed pawns. He will bring his king back next, but to be totally honest he is not that optimistic of being victorious.

☐ Andy	☐ Bob	☐ Carol	☐ Dave	☐ Eddy

Points: ....

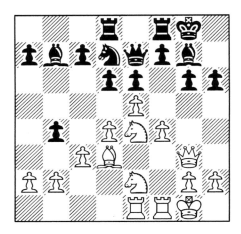

Position after 15...b4

White to move

The white pawn on e5 is a real thorn in Black's position and its compatriot pieces are loitering with intent. How should White set about cracking the black defensive shell?

Andy

Andy's idea is to lure away the black queen from its defensive duties with 16 cxb4. With it out of the way on the queenside (whether Black opts for ...d6xe5 or ...d6-d5) he will then not have enough to cope with a swift invasion of White's forces.

Bob

Though Bob has a self-confessed fondness for h-pawns, here he is particularly attracted to 16 f5. If Black captures with the e-pawn then his queen will suffer whilst 16...gxf5 will leave his king having to face the consequences down the g-file.

Carol

White should simply keep control of the position. Carol sees 16 c4 as an important move. It keeps her strong pawn structure intact and with her e1-rook on the same file as the black queen, a dangerous threat is d4-d5.

Dave

Dave likes the manoeuvre 16 ♗b1 intending 17 ♕d3 and then ♘g3-h5. On h5 the knight couldn't be taken because of the mate on h7 and the knight on h5 would prove to be the final straw.

Eddy

Eddy is fairly calm about the whole situation. He is not ready to panic, but believes that Black should begin to feel nervous after 16 h4. The simple idea is 17 h5 when the defensive cover around the black king will be shown up for what it is: flimsy!

| ☐ Andy | ☐ Bob | ☐ Carol | ☐ Dave | ☐ Eddy |

Points: ....

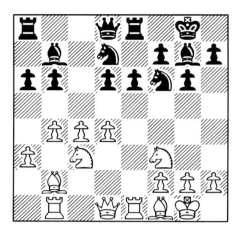

Position after 16...a6

White to move
How should White try to improve his position from here?

Andy
Andy wants to block out Black's light-squared bishop immediately with 17 d5. Not only will this relieve his queen of having to defend the f3-knight, but this steed will also have the opportunity to hop into d4.

Bob
Bob thinks that the bishop has fulfilled its purpose on b2 and wants to set the ball rolling on a new plan: 17 ♗c1. With 18 ♗g5 next his idea is to plan ♕d2 and ♗h6 in order to expose the dark-squared holes around the black king.

Carol

Carol likes a simple plan of vacating any vulnerable pieces from the kingside in order to activate them on the queenside. Specifically she has 17 ♘d2-b3 in mind with the probing a4-a5 up her sleeve. She has an extra pawn on the queenside and a weakening of the a6-pawn could be a decisive factor.

Dave

Eddy wants to play 17 b5. When Black responds with the likely 17...a5, he will pool all of his resources in a giant effort to make the critical break c4-c5. He anticipates that in the long run his b-pawn will prove too hot for Black to handle.

Eddy

Eddy sees the f4-square as a weak point. With 17 g3 he feels that he can kill two birds with one stone by also preparing to reactivate his currently passive light-squared bishop along the g2-b7 diagonal. An eventual favourable trade of bishops will leave White with a nice target on c6.

☐ Andy   ☐ Bob   ☐ Carol   ☐ Dave   ☐ Eddy

Points: ....

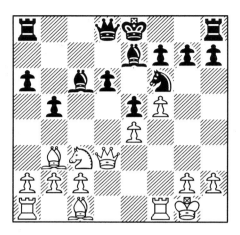

Position after 12...Be7

White to move
Can you suggest a good strategy for White?

Andy
Andy likes the look of 13 h3 with 14 g4 to follow. A kingside pawn storm against the enemy monarch looks very natural.

Bob
Bob also likes the sound of attacking (yes, really!) but suspects that pawns will get in the way here. Black must castle kingside and so there is no reason whatsoever in holding back on 13 ♖f3 with a nice 'swinger' over to g3. This rook will combine well with the lightning bolt ♗h6.

Carol
Carol has spotted a central outpost on d5 and has no hesitation in

recommending 13 ♘d5. If four minor pieces are traded there then the white queen ends up sitting pretty with Black retaining a lousy bishop.

Dave

Dave has seen lots of Open Sicilians like this and in particular he has witnessed White playing b2-b4 on several occasions. This then is his aim with 13 a3 his starter with 14 ♗a2 and then 15 b4 to follow. The idea is ultimately to play ♗b2 when he achieves two raking bishops bearing down on the black king.

Eddy

Just like Carol, Eddy fancies utilising the outpost on d5, but his preference is to finish with a knight on that square. With 13 ♗g5 intending ♗xf6 and then ♗d5 he dreams of reaching an endgame with a good knight on d5 against a bad dark-squared bishop.

☐ Andy	☐ Bob	☐ Carol	☐ Dave	☐ Eddy

Points: ....

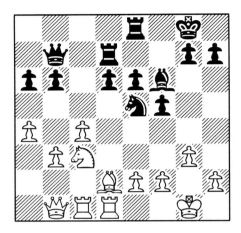

Position after 22 a4

Black to move

White has attempted to set up binds on the usual d5- and b5-squares. Where should Black choose to direct his efforts?

Andy

Andy rates the pawn sacrifice 22...b5. Whichever way White ends up taking this pawn, Black will be able to get in ...d6-d5 for sure and as far as he is concerned to be able to achieve this freeing move is worth a pawn. At the end of the day for once he believes that he is being 100% realistic. To sit back would just allow White to squash him slowly.

Bob

On the kingside according to Bob. It may take a while for his efforts to bear fruit but one has to start somewhere and for him 22...g5 is a good place. He would like to follow this up with ...h7-h5-

h4 when his queen and rook will prove to be superbly placed to join in on an attack along the 2nd rank.

Carol

22...g6 is more Carol's cup of tea. She feels that it's important that she doesn't concede material or ground. The text suggestion protects her f5-pawn should she ever want to play for ...e6-e5 and provides the bishop with a retreat square. Her plan, as is often the case in 'hedgehog' positions, is to sit tight and not make any weakening moves.

Dave

Dave has his mind set on ...d6-d5, but not if it means being left with an isolated pawn. He can double rooks on the d-file, but his star move is 22...♘g6 with ...♘e7 to follow and then, hey presto, the required break!

Eddy

Eddy wants to infiltrate some of White's holes. To improve his own position he has come up with 22...♘c6, intending ...♗d4-c5-b4. He also feels that it's important in this position not to move any of his pawns beyond the third rank as concessions of this type (i.e. squares) could prove very costly.

Now turn to page 129 for the solutions to Test Four.

☐ Andy   ☐ Bob   ☐ Carol   ☐ Dave   ☐ Eddy

Points: ....

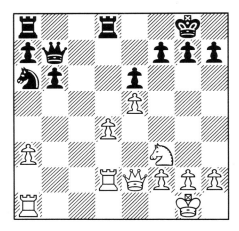

Position after 19 ♖xd2

Black to move

Strong players would say that Black stands better here, but can you recommend a plan for him to try and win the game?

Andy

With the queen on b7 exerting pressure along the a8-h1 diagonal, Andy can see the appeal of getting a knight to f4. Hence he has come up with the manoeuvre 19...♞b8-d7-f8-g6 and even if White prevents ...♞f4, the knight has been improved vastly and is also able to offer any required protection to his own king. Note that all of this takes place in favour of moving the rooks just yet as it isn't clear to him at this moment in time whether they are going to be more constructive on the c- or d-files.

Bob

Bob feels insulted by this whole question, particularly as he reckons that it's much easier for White to try and win the game! However, at a push he suggests 19...g6 intending 20...♔g7 with ...♖h8, ...h7-h5-h4-h3 as being the best way to make inroads against the white king.

Carol

Carol feels that the black knight can obviously be improved by planting it on d5 via c7. The rooks are likely to be traded off (and she is all for that) on the open c-file and the only other thing of importance is that she would like to kick off with 19...h6. This is to cut out 20 ♘g5 not just for its attacking implications, but to prevent ♘e4-d6 as well. Despite all this, the key element for her is likely to be the passed queenside pawn that she can eventually generate.

Dave

As an extremely rare occurrence Dave is suggesting laying all of his cards on the table with 19...b5. He believes that there is no point in faffing around and is advocating pushing his pawn majority before White gets a chance to organise his forces. White must still keep his d-pawn protected and by the time he rallies for a kingside attack Black will have promoted a pawn.

Eddy

Eddy suggests stopping the d-pawn in its tracks with 19...♖d5 and then simply ganging up on it. All three major pieces can hit it on the d-file and ...♘b8-c6 is the icing on the cake. Like Carol though he sees that the long-term future lies with his queenside pawn majority.

☐ Andy	☐ Bob	☐ Carol	☐ Dave	☐ Eddy
Points:				

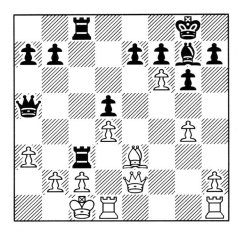

Position after 21...\Rfc8

White to move
In this very tactical middlegame White has several options. Which is his best?

Andy
The amazing 22 fxe7 is Andy's choice. Yes, rather than take either the bishop or the rook he prefers to create the threat of 23 e8♕. In tying one black rook to the back rank Andy believes that he is destined to win material soon anyhow.

Bob
Straight to the point for Bob. After 22 fxg7 ♖xc2+ 23 ♕xc2 ♖xc2+ 24 ♔xc2, despite an extra pawn or two, the black queen will be no match for White's armada of pieces.

Carol

It has to be 22 bxc3 for Carol who gives an absolute priority to eliminating one of the powerful doubled black rooks.

Dave

Dave has decided to ignore both en prise black pieces at the moment in favour of 22 ♔b1. He really likes White's position and wants to avoid a perpetual check.

Eddy

Rather than expose his king position just now, Eddy wants to defend the c2-pawn with 22 ♖d2. This gives his king a safe escape route and, having sorted that situation out, he will then still retain both the f6xg7 and b2xc3 options.

☐ Andy	☐ Bob	☐ Carol	☐ Dave	☐ Eddy
Points:				

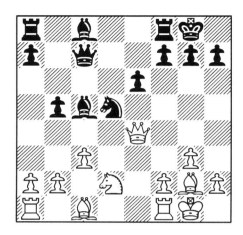

Position after 13...b5

White to move
How should White tackle this position?

Andy
Andy thinks that White should probe the black queenside with 14 a4. As 14...b4 is unplayable because of 15 c4, the end product will include a black isolated queen's pawn.

Bob
To Bob's mind his queenside is solid, but now it's time to get going where it really counts. No pawn storms this time though, as Bob advocates 14 ♘f3 with ♘g5 to follow. With only a knight available to defend his king, Black's days are numbered.

Carol
Carol wants to remain solid and centralised. She will retreat the

queen (14 ♕e2) in order to vacate the e4-square for her knight. Then her dark-squared bishop will be free to enter the action.

Dave

Though ordinarily both sides may have their minds set on just completing their development, Dave has spotted a glitch. 14 ♕d3 will pick up a pawn via 14...a6 15 ♗xd5 exd5 16 ♕xd5. The only way that Black can avoid this is with 14...♕b7 or 14...♕c6, but then 15 a4 really will mean business!

Eddy

Eddy's preference is for 14 c4. This obviously has its sights on budging the d5-knight and if an isolated a-pawn is all that Black is left with on the queenside then all the better.

☐ Andy   ☐ Bob   ☐ Carol   ☐ Dave   ☐ Eddy

Points: ....

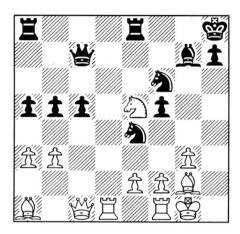

Position after 25...gxf5

White to move

Black has a well placed knight on e4 and a queenside pawn majority. However, he clearly has weaknesses elsewhere. How should White seek to exploit these?

Andy

Andy sees no reason not to just attack Black's weak f5-pawn with 26 ♕f4. If Black opts to defend it with 26...♕c8 then 27 ♘f7+-h6+ will turn the screws.

Bob

Bob believes that 26 g4 is the way to wrap things up. Not so much with an attacking slant here, his intention is simply to undermine the protection of the e4-knight. Black is unable to capture on g4 with the pawn because of 27 ♗xe4, or with the knight because of 27 f3.

Carol

Carol wants to retreat her attacked knight to f3 from where she can soon relocate it to h4. She has singled out Black's f5-pawn as his main weakness and her suggestion seems just right to exploit it.

Dave

Dave wants to make the e5-square an outpost for his knight with 26 f4. Yes, he has observed that it drops a pawn to 26...♞xg3, but his rather colourful idea includes 27 ♖fe1 intending ♔f2 and ♖h1 with a strong attack along the h-file.

Eddy

26 ♞d3 is Eddy's choice. Whilst hitting c5, White also ensures that Black's f-pawn won't be able to liquidate itself via ...f5-f4. The text also has the advantage of unleashing the a1-bishop.

□ Andy	□ Bob	□ Carol	□ Dave	□ Eddy
Points:				

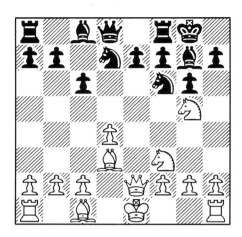

Position after 8...0-0

White to move

Arguably White has a slight edge, but can you suggest a plan that will ultimately put his opponent's solid-looking position under serious pressure?

Andy

Rather than make a decision just yet as to which side to castle, Andy wants to plough straight ahead with 9 ♘e5. It's undoubtedly a great square for the knight and the beautiful thing is that he can support it with ♘g5-f3 when this otherwise awkwardly placed knight is attacked by ...h7-h6.

Bob

Bob observes that it was about time that another position like this came up. For him 9 h4 is the most testing. White threatens 10 h5 and his intention is to meet 9...h6 with 10 h5 anyway. He anticipates a knight sacrifice on e6 or f7 a bit later too!

Carol
Carol believes that White should build up slowly and play the 'containing' game. 9 0-0 must come first with the blunting 10 c3 likely to be next. If attacked her g5-knight will return to e4 and she will eventually seek to pressurise Black along the e-file.

Dave
Dave recognises the fact that a kingside attack is White's most promising option but believes that he should complete his development first before razzing his h-pawn down the board. His choice is 9 ♗d2 with 10 0-0-0 up next.

Eddy
Like Carol (not much chance of them dating if opposites attract!) Eddy is sticking with general opening principles and castling early. However, after 9 0-0 he likes the look of c2-c4 to take away the d5-square from a black knight and the real pressure will come with an expansion of his queenside pawns.

☐ Andy   ☐ Bob   ☐ Carol   ☐ Dave   ☐ Eddy

Points: ....

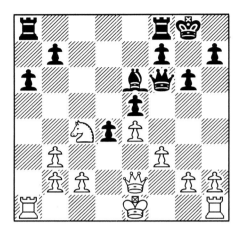

Position after 18 ♘c4

Black to move
Should Black continue simply in order to achieve a victory or does he need that little bit more invention?

Andy
Andy thinks that Black needs to be a touch adventurous here. He is attracted to a course of action along the c-file but considers that the c2-pawn alone is not a significant enough weakness for White to lose the game. Hence his idea is to eke out another concession or two and 18...h5-h4-h3 is just the ticket for Andy.

Bob
18...g5 and 19...g4 is what Bob has in mind. Ultimately White will either be left with an isolated e-pawn or a half-open g-file. If he castles short then Black expects to hammer his opponent down the g-file whilst long castling will run into grief along the c-file.

Carol

18...♗xc4 19 bxc4 ♖ac8 is Carol's preference when she believes that through uncomplicated play she is likely to pick up one of White's c-pawns.

Dave

Dave believes that it's essential that Black's f-pawn is brought into the equation in order to reap maximum benefit from this position. For him 18...♕g7 is a good start.

Eddy

The c-file is everything for Eddy. He feels no compulsion to concede his bishop for the knight yet, but expects a simple doubling of rooks on the c-file to eventually bring forth the reward of a pawn.

☐ Andy   ☐ Bob ·   ☐ Carol   ☐ Dave   ☐ Eddy

Points: ....

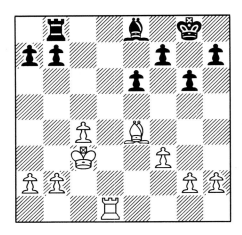

Position after 21...♗e8

White to move

White has a queenside pawn majority and a more active king. How should he attack this ending?

Andy

Andy wants to waste no time in advancing his pawn majority. A simple plan beginning with 22 c5 and including b2-b4, ♖a1, a2-a4 and b4-b5 is what he has in mind. Almost certainly the outcome will be that Black has to concede his bishop for the inevitable created passed pawn.

Bob

Bob hardly feels that the word 'attack' is applicable here. However, he has spotted the opportunity to go walkabout with his king. 22 ♖d6 followed by a king march up to f6 is what Bob has in mind when he feels that Black will be powerless to respond.

Carol

Carol wants to push her majority on the queenside but acknowledges that Black will have plans for his kingside pawns. For this reason she would like to implement the restrictive 22 f4 first.

Dave

Dave has his mind set on invading the 7th rank and in order to do this he must eliminate Black's bishop. His plan is 22 ♔b4 followed by 23 ♗c2-a4. Even if Black's king makes it over in time to prevent ♖d7, it will be cut off along the d-file and thus unable to deal with the queenside passed pawn that White will create.

Eddy

Eddy wants to bind Black's kingside. His master plan involves fixing a white pawn on g5 and then planting his king on e5. Unable to make progress with his own kingside pawns, Black will have nothing better to do than just sit back and watch White's c-pawn approach touchdown!

☐ Andy	☐ Bob	☐ Carol	☐ Dave	☐ Eddy

Points: ....

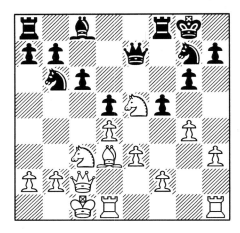

Position after 14...0-0

White to move

White has a superbly placed knight on e5, but how should he seek to make progress from here?

Andy

As usual in these Queen's Gambit Declined positions a minority attack is the right path for White. Andy concedes that such a theme is tricky with his king castled queenside, but nevertheless is somewhat taken by 15 ♔b1-a1 with ♖b1 and b2-b4-b5 to follow. Once b5xc6 is achieved he believes that the black position will collapse.

Bob

Queenside play is out of the question for Bob who advocates 15 f4 followed by 16 h4-h5. He is naturally delighted that these are his two favourite moves with his other, g2-g4, already having been played. Oh, did I forget to mention that he's after an all-out kingside attack?

Carol

Carol wants to limit the activity of the black pieces. She likes 15 ♔b1 and with ♖c1 and ♕e2 to follow she fancies a doubling rooks on the c-file plan. There is little doubt then that Black won't dare consider the likes of ...c6-c5 or ...b7-b5, so White will be free to begin slow but steady motions on the kingside.

Dave

Dave wants to pre-empt Black's queenside play with the cheeky 15 a4. Before Black gets in ...a5-a4 he wants to achieve a4-a5 himself, which will kick away the b6-knight and pave the way for ♘a4-c5.

Eddy

Eddy wants to centralise. His natural plan includes playing the two moves ♖he1 and f2-f3 (actually any order will do) and his aim is to achieve the e3-e4 break in the centre.

☐ Andy	☐ Bob	☐ Carol	☐ Dave	☐ Eddy
Points:				

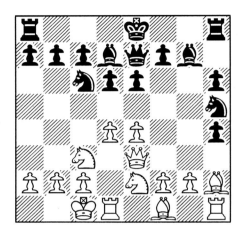

Position after 12...gxh4

White to move
Black is 'half' a pawn up. How should White deal with this situation?

Andy
With the black king in the centre of the board, Andy is logically advocating opening things up with 13 d5. Following this 13...exd5 14 ♘xd5 will be very awkward for Black whilst 13...♘e5 will enable White to improve the position of his knight immeasurably with 14 ♘d4.

Bob
It's clear to Bob that Black is going to have to castle queenside. Hence he wants to get things ready for the big push. He accepts that Rome wasn't built in a day and so suggests starting with 13 a3. This is hardly a giant step for mankind, but 14 b4 will be a bigger one and it could be the same old story (actually Bob is predicting

it!).

Carol

A simple and promising plan according to Carol is to try and regain the pawn as soon as possible. With 13 ♗g1 intending 14 g4, 15 f3 and 16 ♗f2 she is likely to do just that after which she will be left with a clear structural advantage.

Dave

'Deviously simple!' exclaims Dave. I'm not sure that's possible, but there certainly seems to be some logic to his straightforward plan of 13 ♔b1 and 14 ♘c1. The knight will have options on b3 but more to the point White will have enabled ♗e2 hitting the h5-knight and thus regaining the h4-pawn.

Eddy

Eddy wants to leave his dark-squared bishop where it is for the time being, but is eager to regain the pawn as quickly as possible. His neat idea is 13 ♘g1-f3xh4. The knight may end up temporarily a little offside, but the resulting structural edge will be more lasting.

☐ Andy	☐ Bob ·	☐ Carol	☐ Dave	☐ Eddy

Points: ....

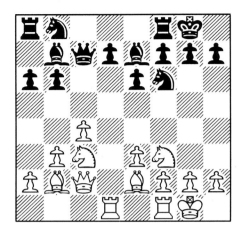

Position after 12...0-0

White to move

Hedgehog positions are notoriously difficult to break down. What advice would you offer to White here in tackling this one?

Andy

According to Andy, White should seek to hassle the f6-knight before Black manages to complete his development. Irregular though it may seem, his solution is 13 h3, intending 14 g4-g5.

Bob

In his true inimitable style, Bob is opting for a kingside attack! Though not advocating a pawn storm this time, he is attracted to 13 ♘g5. Gunning unsubtly for h7, he has observed that 13...h6 loses to 14 ♘d5 and that this stylish move may figure soon anyhow.

Carol

Carol wants to move forward slowly (but surely). She suggests keeping a bind on the d5-square and after 13 e4 she would drop her knight into d4 and then utilise the vacated square for the b7-bishop blunting f2-f3.

Dave

Although there is no longer a rook on a1, Dave still thinks that the queenside probing 13 a4-a5 is good value for money. The certain outcome is one or two isolated a-pawn(s) for Black and this lasting weakness looks grim compared to White's ultra-solid structure.

Eddy

Eddy quite simply wants to double his rooks on the d-file. Though his aim is to make life hell for Black's d7-pawn, he accepts that it may be a long time before he actually wins it. However, a big bonus as far as he is concerned is that his plan has the advantage of dissuading ...d7-d5.

Now turn to page 136 for the solutions to Test Five.

☐ Andy	☐ Bob	☐ Carol	☐ Dave	☐ Eddy

Points: ....

Solutions To Test One

Solution 1-1

The knight on h5 proves to be a big stumbling block as far as a kingside attack is concerned. 15 g4 would allow the knight to plonk itself on f4 as White is rarely advised to swap off his good bishop for it even if it means winning a pawn. Indeed the pawn in question here would be Black's e-pawn whose presence is currently hindering the King's Indian bishop. Trading off his good bishop for this piece with a ♗h6 makes little sense for White anyhow as Black could defend any unlikely attack along the 2nd rank by advancing his f-pawn and using his queen.

Andy offers the best plan. It isn't so risky advancing the pawns around the white king as Black has no way of exploiting this. His pieces are unable to enter the white position on the kingside and the following encounter demonstrates how White is able to utilise his space advantage: 15 b4!? a5 16 cxd6 cxd6 17 b5 ♖fc8 18 ♔b2 ♕e8 19 a4 b6 20 ♖c1 ♕e7 21 ♘b1 f5 22 ♖c6

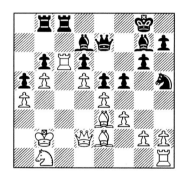

22...♗xc6 23 dxc6 fxe4 24 fxe4 ♘f6 25 ♘c3 ♔h8 26 ♗g5 ♕c7 27 ♗xf6 ♗xf6 28 ♗g4 ♗g7 29 ♘d5 ♕d8 30 ♗xc8 ♖xc8 31 ♕f2 ♕g5 32 h4 ♕h5 33 ♕f3 ♕h6 34 ♕e3 ♕h5 35 ♘xb6 ♖f8 36 c7 ♗h6 37 ♕f3 ♖xf3 38 gxf3 ♕xf3 39 c8♕+ ♗f8 40 ♖c1 d5 41 ♕xf8+ ♕xf8 42 ♖c8 1-0 Ward-G.Gibbs, Caribbean Open 1999.

Points:

Andy	10
Bob	2
Carol	2
Dave	2
Eddy	2

Solution 1-2

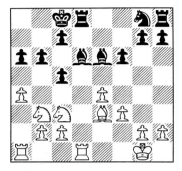

The Spanish (Ruy Lopez) Exchange Variation does have a reputation of being rather dull, but this encounter livened up quickly thanks to the recommendation of **Bob** (and obviously the ex-World Champion!). You can't exactly fault Carol's sensible suggestion, but Black will complete his development and if things open up his bishop pair will definitely have a positive influence. The continuation 14 a5 ♔b7 15 e5

(see following diagram)

15...♗e7 16 ♖xd8 ♗xd8 17 ♘e4 ♔c6 18 axb6 cxb6 19 ♘bxc5 ♗c8 20 ♘xa6 fxe5 21 ♘b4+ 1-0 was Fischer-Spassky, Belgrade (match) 1992. I'm not sure that Bob had

seen all this, but it's his plan that gets maximum points nonetheless!

Points:

Andy	2
Bob	10
Carol	5
Dave	1
Eddy	1

Solution 1-3

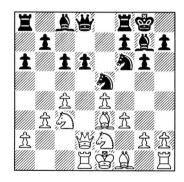

Eddy's choice was the same as the World Champion's in what must surely have been one of Anatoly Karpov's most humiliating experiences. Indeed after 11...b5! 12 cxb5 axb5 13 ♕xd6 ♘fd7 14 f4 b4 15

♘b1 ♞g4 16 ♗d4 ♗xd4 17 ♕xd4 ♖xa2 18 h3 c5 19 ♕g1 White soon found himself with all of his pieces on the back rank.

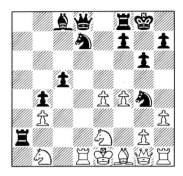

19...♞gf6 20 e5 ♞e4 21 h4 c4 22 ♞c1 c3 23 ♞xa2 c2 24 ♕d4 cxd1♕+ 25 ♔xd1 ♞dc5 26 ♕xd8 ♖xd8+ 27 ♔c2 ♞f2 0-1 Karpov-Kasparov, Linares 1993. There is little doubt that 11...b5! was the start of a good active plan.

Points:

Andy	2
Bob	0
Carol	1
Dave	0
Eddy	10

Solution 1-4

With the exception of Andy's rather optimistic view, there are many plausible points in all of the plans. However, one should not underestimate Black's position. Sure, he has doubled pawns, but a ...c7-c5 break will no doubt be up his sleeve and the use of the d5-

square is helpful too.

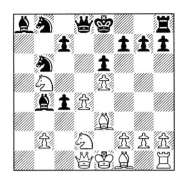

The most accurate plan was suggested by **Dave**: 13 ♕g4! 0-0 14 ♗e2 (perhaps the obvious 14 ♗h6 would be good too, but the enforced exchange sacrifice 14...g6 could prove okay as it's White's dark-squared bishop that is holding his centre together) 14...♔h8 15 0-0 ♞c6 16 ♞xc4 ♞xc4 17 ♗xc4 ♗a5 18 ♗g5 ♕d7 19 ♕h4 ♞b4 20 ♖a1 ♕c6 21 ♗f1 ♕b6 22 ♖a3!

Here Black resigned in Gormally-Krush, Millennium Masters, Oakham 2000, as there is no defence to 23 ♖h3.

Points:

Andy	1
Bob	2
Carol	2
Dave	10
Eddy	3

Solution 1-5

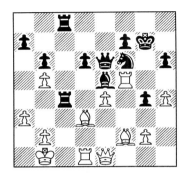

Black sealed victory with 30...♖c3! Just as **Bob** said, 30...♖a4 with the same ...♖xa3 idea would also have been successful, the ultimate intention as in this game to get the queen to b3. The game continued 31 ♖xe5 dxe5 32 bxc3 ♕b3+ 33 ♔a1 ♕xa3+ 34 ♔b1 ♕b3+ 35 ♔a1 ♖xc3

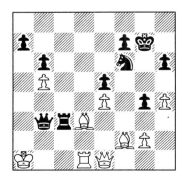

36 ♗b1 ♕a3+ 37 ♗a2 ♖c2 0-1 Van Wely-Adams, Wijk aan Zee 1998.

Points:

Andy	0
Bob	10
Carol	2
Dave	0
Eddy	1

Solution 1-6

The problem with Dave's plan is that Black is not forced to meet 18 exf5 with 18...♗xf3 as 18...♖xf5 is perfectly reasonable. Eddy has a nice idea, but his a4-knight is a long way from d5. **Bob** once again found the most convincing continuation as demonstrated by a young rising star: 18 ♗c4+ ♔h8 19 g6! h6 20 ♗xh6!

(see following diagram)

20...fxe4 21 ♖dg1 e3 22 ♕xe3 d5 23 ♗xg7+! ♔xg7 24 h6+ ♔f6 25 g7 dxc4 26 h7 1-0 Morozevich-Rowson, Birmingham (4NCL) 2000.

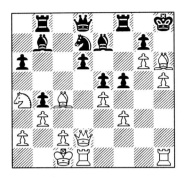

Points:

Andy	2
Bob	10
Carol	2
Dave	2
Eddy	2

Solution 1-7

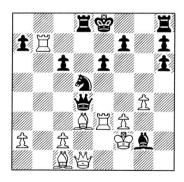

Bob was too cocky and made an obvious error in his analysis because of course 21 ♖xe6+ is illegal. **Andy** though is spot on: 21 ♗g6!! ♘e7 (21...♕xd1 22 ♖xe6+ ♔f8 23 ♗xh6+ ♔g8 24 ♗xf7+ is mate!)

(see following diagram)

22 ♕xd4 ♖xd4 23 ♖d3 ♖d8 24

♖xd8+ ♔xd8 25 ♗d3 1-0 Anand-Lautier, Biel 1997.

Points:

Andy	10
Bob	0
Carol	2
Dave	1
Eddy	1

Solution 1-8

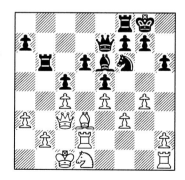

Cautious she may be, but **Carol** is obviously one for a good long-term plan. Indeed many people's favourite to be the next World Champion now employed just this suggestion and boy did things turn out well!

The game finished 18...♖fb8 19 ♗c2 ♕b7 20 ♖e1 ♘h7 21 ♖e3 ♕a6 22 ♗d3 ♗d7 23 ♗f1 ♘g5 24 ♖ed3 ♘e6 25 ♘e3 ♘d4 26 ♘d5 ♖b3

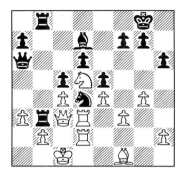

0-1 Ljubojevic-Kramnik, Monaco (blindfold) 2000. Yes, all this with his eyes closed!

Points:

Andy	0
Bob	0
Carol	10
Dave	1
Eddy	1

Solution 1-9

Eddy has the best plan and indeed after 19...♗f8! 20 a3 c5 21 dxc5 ♖xc5 22 ♖xc5 ♕xc5 23 ♕xc5 ♗xc5 the desired affect of opening up the position for the bishops had also been achieved. The game continued 24 ♖c1 ♖c8 25 ♗f4 ♔f7 26 b4 ♗f8 27 ♖xc8 ♗xc8 28 ♘d2 e5 29 ♗e3 a6 30 ♔f1 ♔e6 31 f4 exf4 32 ♗xf4 ♔d5

33 ♗e3 ♗d7 34 ♔e2 ♗d6 35 h3 ♗b5+ 36 ♔f3 ♗e5 37 ♘e4 ♗b2 38 ♗d2 f5 39 ♘c3+ ♔c4 40 ♘xb5 axb5 41 g4 fxg4+ 42 ♔xg4 ♗xa3 43 ♔g5 ♗xb4 44 ♗f4 ♗f8 45 ♔f6 b4 46 ♔f7 b3 47 ♗e5 ♗b4 0-1 Giddins-Emms, Isle of Man 1999. Note that Bob's 19...e5 is positionally feeble. At best it swaps off White's isolated d-pawn and leaves Black with three isolated pawns!

Points:

Andy	0
Bob	0
Carol	1
Dave	0
Eddy	10

Solution 1-10

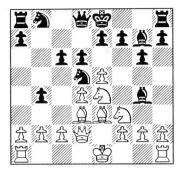

An ambitious but nevertheless justified attacking plan initiated by 10 ♗h6 was employed by English Grandmaster Nigel Short. After 10...0-0 11 h4! (as recommended by *Dave*) 11...♗xf3 12 gxf3 dxe5 13 h5, preparing to allow a crushing queen and rook alliance down the h-file, proved extremely dangerous:

(see following diagram)

13...♗f6 14 ♘xf6+ exf6 15 hxg6 fxg6 16 ♗xf8 ♕xf8 17 dxe5 ♘d7 18 ♗e4 ♘7b6 19 exf6 ♕xf6 20 ♕h6 ♕f7 21 0-0-0 ♘f6 22 ♗xg6 1-0 Short-Irzhanov, Elista Olympiad 1998.

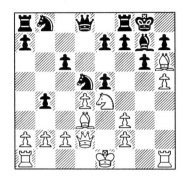

Points:

Andy	1
Bob	0
Carol	3
Dave	10
Eddy	2

Solutions To Test Two

Solution 2-1

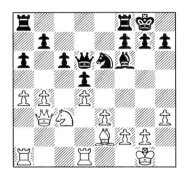

Play in this game continued with 16...b5 17 ♖ac1 ♖fb8 18 ♘a2 ♖c8 19 ♖c2 ♖c7 20 ♘c1 ♘g5 21 ♘d3 ♗e7 22 ♖dc1 f5 23 f4 ♘e4 24 ♗f3 ♘f6 25 ♖a1 ♕d8 26 ♘e5 ♖ac8 27 axb5 axb5 28 ♖a6 ♕d6 29 ♖c5 when too much pressure built up on Black's queenside and he was destined to drop a pawn: 29...♕e6 30 ♖xb5 ♗d6 31 ♖bb6 ♗xe5 32 fxe5 ♘e4 33 ♗xe4 fxe4 34 b5 ♔f7 35 ♖xc6 ♖xc6 36 bxc6 ♖c7 37 ♕b8 ♕e7 38 ♖b6 1-0 Ward-Czibulka, Malta 2000. The point is that Black never looked like getting the knight to the desired c4-square. With **Dave's** plan the position would have taken on a completely different complexion. Playing White in the game I was certainly far more worried by the prospect of 16...♗d8! 17 b5 ♗c7 18 g3 ♘g5 19 h4 ♘h3+ 20 ♔g2 ♘xf2

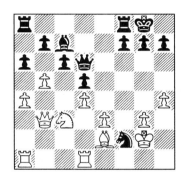

21 ♔xf2 ♕xg3+ 22 ♔f1 ♕h3+ 23 ♔e1 ♕xe3. Of course there are other ways for White to defend, but it's not as though there are many pieces around his king rushing to help out.

Points:

Andy	2
Bob	0
Carol	0
Dave	10
Eddy	1

Solution 2-2

I recall the following comeback game inciting much excitement. Could the one and only Bobby Fischer once again impose himself on world chess? Sadly the promise of this game was never quite realised.

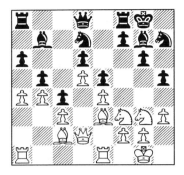

Perhaps it's not a perfect example, but the extravagant concept advocated by **Dave** was set to be successful until Spassky deemed it necessary to sacrifice in order to give himself something to do. True, it's not surprising that with White's pieces offside, Black gained some counterplay, but White was able to regroup in order to gain the full point: 22 ♖a3 ♘df6 23 ♖ea1 ♕d7 24 ♖1a2 ♖fc8 25 ♕c1 ♗f8 26 ♕a1

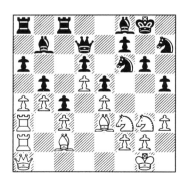

26...♕e8 27 ♘f1 ♗e7 28 ♘1d2 ♔g7

29 ♘b1 ♘xe4 30 ♗xe4 f5 31 ♗c2 ♗xd5 32 axb5 axb5 33 ♖a7 ♔f6 34 ♘bd2 ♖xa7 35 ♖xa7 ♖a8 36 g4 hxg4 37 hxg4 ♖xa7 38 ♕xa7 f4 39 ♗xf4 exf4 40 ♘h4 ♗f7 41 ♕d4+ ♔e6 42 ♘f5 ♗f8 43 ♕xf4 ♔d7 44 ♘d4 ♕e1+ 45 ♔g2 ♗d5+ 46 ♗e4 ♗xe4+ 47 ♘xe4 ♗e7 48 ♘xb5 ♘f8 49 ♘bxd6 ♘e6 50 ♕e5 1-0 Fischer-Spassky, Sveti Stefan/Belgrade (match) 1992.

Note that playing f2-f4 will only donate Black the e5-square after ...e5xf4.

Points:

Andy	1
Bob	1
Carol	1
Dave	10
Eddy	3

Solution 2-3

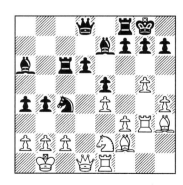

In fact 23...♘a3+ may well do the business (not mate straightaway, but certainly lasting pressure). However the maximum 10 points goes to the thematic 23...d5! Kasparov's choice (advocated by **Eddy**) simply blew White away: 24 exd5 ♖d6 25 f4 ♖xd5 26 ♖d3 ♘a3+!

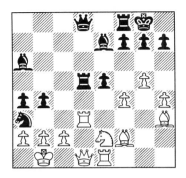

27 bxa3 ♗xd3 28 cxd3 ♖xd3 0-1 Topalov-Kasparov, Amsterdam 1995.

Points:

Andy	1
Bob	6
Carol	0
Dave	2
Eddy	10

Solution 2-4

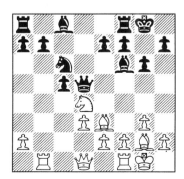

The up and coming English International Master concluded a very nice

game after deciding that he could snatch the pawn on a2: 12...♕xa2! 13 ♖a1 ♕b2 14 ♖b1 ♕a3 15 ♖a1 ♕b4 16 ♖b1 ♘xd4 17 ♖xb4 cxb4 18 ♗xd4 ♗xd4 19 ♕a4 a5 20 ♖b1 ♗c3 21 ♗d5 e6 22 ♗c4 ♖d8 23 ♗b5 ♖d5 24 e4 ♖xb5! 25 ♕xb5 a4

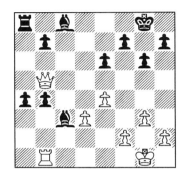

26 e5 a3 27 d4 a2 28 ♖a1 ♗xa1 29 ♕e8+ ♔g7 30 ♕d8 ♗d7 31 ♕xa8 b3 32 ♕d8 b2 33 ♕f6+ ♔g8 34 ♕d8+ ♗e8 0-1 Norris-Gormally, Millennium Masters, Oakham 2000. **Andy** was spot on.

Points:

Andy	10
Bob	0
Carol	2
Dave	1
Eddy	0

Solution 2-5

The white knight is a fair distance from e4 and this factor no doubt had a big influence in the top English Grandmaster's decision to adopt an almost caveman-like approach (yep, **Bob** is the man for the job!):

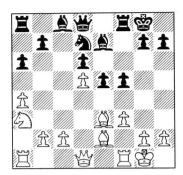

14...f4!? 15 ♗f2 ♕e8 16 ♘c4 ♕h5
17 ♔h1 ♖f6

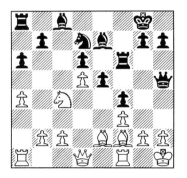

18 g4 fxg3 19 ♗xg3 ♖g6 20 f4 ♕h6
21 ♕e1 ♘f6 22 fxe5 ♘e4 23 ♖a3
♖xg3 24 ♖xg3 ♗h4 25 ♖gf3 ♗g4
26 ♖3f2 ♘xf2+ 27 ♖xf2 ♗xf2 28
♕xf2 ♖f8 29 ♕e1 ♕h3 0-1 Rowson-
Adams, London 1998. With the exception of Dave's dubious pawn
sacrifice, though, they were all
pretty reasonable suggestions.

Points:

Andy	4
Bob	10
Carol	3
Dave	0
Eddy	2

Solution 2-6

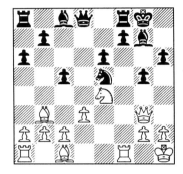

Bob obviously shares certain traits
with the last World Championship
challenger(!) as Anand also selected
17 ♗xg5!? hxg5 18 ♘xg5 ♘g6 19
♖ae1 ♕e7 20 ♖f5 ♗f6 21 ♘xe6
fxe6? 22 ♖xe6!

22...♔g7 23 ♖xe7+ ♗xe7 24 ♖xf8
♗xf8 25 h4 1-0 Anand-Gelfand,

Wijk aan Zee 1996. Of course, 21...fxe6? was a mistake, but even after the best defence 21...♖e8 22 ♖e4 ♗xe6 23 ♗xe6 fxe6 24 ♕xg6+♗g7 25 ♖f3 White's active pieces will provide him with enough for a draw. Eddy was right about 17 ♘xc5 but there is not enough time for his plan as Black will no doubt put his kingside majority to good use through a timely expansion.

Points:

Andy	0
Bob	10
Carol	3
Dave	2
Eddy	0

Solution 2-7

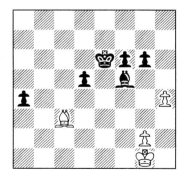

In a stroke of genius here Grand-master Alexei Shirov found an amazing move. Demonstrating the same sort of ambition as *Andy*(!), Shirov now gave priority to offering his king the fast track f5-e4. After 47...♗h3!! 48 gxh3 he also didn't have to worry about dropping the f6-pawn as White's now doubled h-pawns pose no real threat. The game continued 48...f5 49 ♔f2 ♔e4 50 ♗xf6 d4 51 ♗e7 ♔d3 52 ♗c5 ♔c4 53 ♗e7 ♔b3

0-1 Topalov-Shirov, Linares 1998. Now 54 ♔e2 would be met by 54...♔c2 when the white bishop would be overworked controlling d2 and halting the rampant a-pawn. This was the only way to win. Bob would soon run out of pawns to promote with his suggestion whilst the others would allow White to set up a dark-squared blockade on d4 and a1 with the adequate defensive combination of king and bishop.

Points:

Andy	10
Bob	0
Carol	1
Dave	1
Eddy	1

Solution 2-8

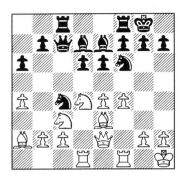

Perhaps **Carol** should consider a change in her opening repertoire! The following controlled encounter is a joy to watch: 15 ♗c1! ♖fd8 16 g4! ♕c5 17 g5 ♘e8 18 f5 e5 19 ♘d5

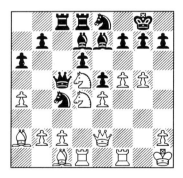

19...♗f8 20 b4 ♕a7 21 ♗xc4 exd4 22 g6 ♔h8 23 gxf7 ♘c7 24 ♘f4 1-0 Emms-Shipov, Hastings Premier 1999. The unstoppable threat is 25 ♘g6+ when the white queen will swoop to deliver mate on the h-file.

Points:

Andy	1
Bob	0
Carol	10
Dave	0
Eddy	2

Solution 2-9

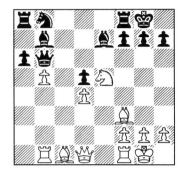

Carol's choice is the first idea that came to the Indian Grandmaster. However, in his own words he then decided that a re-routing of his light-squared bishop could be even more to the point. When **Eddy** implied that he would have reasonable chances for a kingside attack with his light-squared bishop on d3, he wasn't wrong! The game continued 17 ♗e2! axb5 18 ♖xb5 ♕c7 19 ♗f4 ♗d6 20 ♗d3 ♗a6 21 ♗xh7+!

(see following diagram)

21...♔xh7 22 ♕h5+ ♔g8 23 ♖b3 ♗xe5 24 ♖h3 f6 25 dxe5 ♕e7 26 ♕h7+ ♔f7 27 ♖g3 ♔e8 28 ♖xg7 ♕e6 29 exf6 ♘c6 30 ♖a1 ♔d8 31 h4 ♗b7 32 ♖c1 ♗a6 33 ♖a1 ♗b7 34 ♖d1 ♗a6 35 ♕b1 ♖xf6 36 ♗g5 1-0 Anand-Karpov, Las Palmas 1996.

120

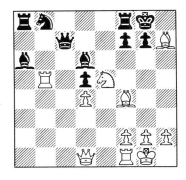

Points:

Andy	2
Bob	0
Carol	4
Dave	1
Eddy	10

Solution 2-10

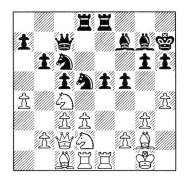

Yes, it's probably fair to say that there wasn't a great selection of plans to choose from. A queenside squeeze starting with 21...a6 and

aiming for ...b6-b5 looks very reasonable, but take a look at the highly instructive: 21...♘db4!? 22 cxb4 ♘xb4 23 ♕b1 ♘xd3 24 ♖e2 e4 25 b3 ♗d4 26 ♘f1 a6 27 ♗e3 b5 28 axb5 axb5 29 ♘cd2 ♗f6 30 ♕c2 c4 31 bxc4 bxc4 32 ♘b1 ♖b8 33 ♘c3 ♖b2

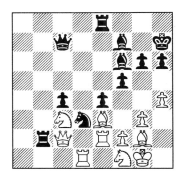

34 ♕xb2 ♘xb2 35 ♖xb2 ♗xc3 36 ♖c2 ♗g7 37 ♗d4 ♖d8 38 ♖cd2 ♖xd4 39 ♖xd4 ♗xd4 40 ♖xd4 c3 41 ♖d1 ♗b3 42 ♖c1 c2 43 ♘e3 ♕c3 44 ♘xc2 ♗xc2 45 ♗f1 e3 46 h5 ♕d2 0-1 Salov-Gelfand, Hoogovens (blitz) 1998. This was just a blitz game but 21...♘db4 was a great judgement call by Gelfand and *Andy*!

Points:

Andy	10
Bob	1
Carol	1
Dave	0
Eddy	0

Solutions To Test Three

Solution 3-1

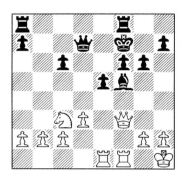

Unfortunately this was one of my own games. Having held a significant edge, as White I now had the blinkers on and was unable to accept that I was no longer better. I continued 19 g4? and should have lost quicker: 19...♗xg4 20 ♕xf6+ ♔g8 21 ♕g5 ♗f3+ 22 ♔g1 ♖f4

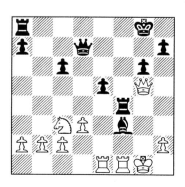

23 ♕xe5 ♖g4+ 24 ♔f2 ♖f8 25 ♔e3 ♖e8 26 ♕xe8+ ♕xe8+ 27 ♔xf3 ♕d7 28 ♘e4 ♔g7 29 ♖f2 ♖h4 30 ♔e3 c5 31 ♔d2 c4 32 ♘f6 ♕b7 33 ♖ee2 cxd3 34 cxd3 ♕xb2+ 35 ♔e1 ♕c1 mate Ward-Hennigan, Birmingham (4NCL) 2000. I was foolish to open up my king in this manner and I should have taken the sensible advice offered by *Carol*.

Points:

Andy	0
Bob	0
Carol	10
Dave	0
Eddy	2

Solution 3-2

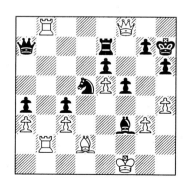

There is no mate for Black after 45...♘e3+ 46 ♗xe3 ♕xe3 as the

122

white rook defends adequately along the second rank. Also 45...♗g4 is foiled by 46 ♔g2, but instead in a memorable encounter Nigel Short correctly assessed that his opponent's position was kind of paralysed. As observed by **Eddy**, there is no defence to the innovative march of the black king into white territory whilst the black rook holds the fort at the back. Rather than suffer the indignation of the enemy monarch just coming down and picking off his g-pawn, the World Champion attempted a distraction, but he lost quickly anyhow: 45...♔g6! 46 ♗c1 ♔h5 47 ♖a8 ♕c5

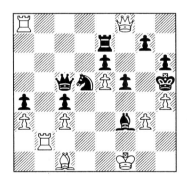

48 ♖c8 ♕xa3 49 g4+ ♗xg4 50 ♖xc4 ♕a1 0-1 Kasparov-Short, London (rapidplay) 1987.

Points:

Andy	2
Bob	0
Carol	2
Dave	2
Eddy	10

Solution 3-3

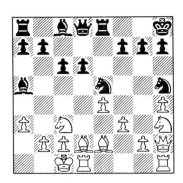

It's worth noting that 14...♕xh4? 15 ♘g5 ♕xh2 16 ♖xh2 ♘f6 17 ♘xh7 is crushing for White who is definitely threatening 15 g4. Karpov and **Dave** had it right as became clear after 14...♗xh3! 15 ♕xh3 ♗xc3 16 bxc3 ♘f6 17 c4 ♕b6 18 f4 ♘ed7 19 ♗d3 ♘c5 20 e5 ♘a4 21 ♗b4 dxe5 22 c5 ♕c7 23 ♗c4 a5

0-1 Shirov-Karpov, Dos Hermanas 1995. The bishop pair is always a good thing, but the black king remained safe whilst its enemy number was exposed due to a wretched pawn structure.

Points:

Andy	1
Bob	2
Carol	0
Dave	10
Eddy	0

Solution 3-4

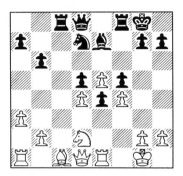

I like the idea of invading White's light-squared holes on the queen-side and the knight would be well placed on e6. I'm not sure I fancy the rook on e8 though and I have gone with *Carol*. White could have defended better but the rest of the game is instructive nonetheless. A smooth exchange sacrifice leads to a couple of wicked passed pawns: 18...♞b8 19 ♞b1 ♞c6 20 ♞c3?! ♞xd4!

(see following diagram)

21 ♗e3 ♖c4 22 ♔h1 ♗c5 23 ♖c1 a5 24 b3 ♖xc3 25 ♖xc3 ♞e6 26 ♗c1 d4 27 ♖h3 g6 28 ♖e2 ♛d5 29 b4 axb4 30 axb4 ♗xb4 31 ♖b3 ♛c4 32 ♖b1 ♖c8 33 h3 d3 34 ♖f2 ♗c5 35

♖f1 e3 36 ♗xe3 ♗xe3 37 ♖f3 ♛d4 38 ♛b3 ♔f7 39 ♖d1 ♖c3 40 ♛b1 d2 41 g3 ♖c1 42 ♛b3 ♛e4 43 ♔g2 ♖xd1 0-1 McDonald-Gormally, Millennium Masters, Oakham 2000.

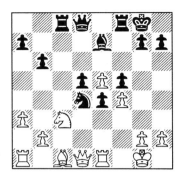

Points:

Andy	1
Bob	1
Carol	10
Dave	4
Eddy	2

Solution 3-5

I was particularly proud of this game and believe I was right to continue in the manner advocated

by **Dave**. Indeed after 24 e5! dxe5
25 d6 exd6 26 ♘e4

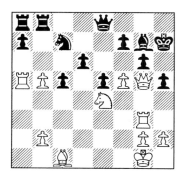

in view of the multiple threats that
the powerful white knight gener-
ated (e.g. capturing on d6 thus de-
flecting the black queen from its
vital task of supporting g6), the
English superstar decided to hit
the emergency button. Ultimately
though this was to no avail:
26...♘e6 27 fxe6 ♕xe6 28 ♕d2
♔g8 29 ♘g5 ♕c4 30 ♖c3 ♕d4+ 31
♕xd4 exd4 32 ♖f3 ♖b7 33 ♘e4
♗f8 34 ♗f4 ♖d8 35 ♗g5 ♖db8 36
♘f6+ ♔g7 37 ♘d5 ♖xb5 38 ♖xa7
♖5b7 39 ♗f6+ ♔h7 40 ♖xb7 ♖xb7
41 b3 ♗g7 42 h4 ♔g8 43 ♔f2 ♔f8
44 ♗xg7+ ♔xg7 45 ♔e2 ♖b8 46
♔d2 ♖e8 47 ♔d3 ♖e5 48 ♘f6 ♖e6
49 ♘e4 f5 50 ♘g5 ♖e5 51 g3 ♔f6
52 ♔c4 ♔e7 53 b4 ♔d7 54 b5 ♔c7
55 ♖a3 ♖e1 56 ♖a7+ ♔b6 57 ♖a6+
♔b7 58 ♘f7 d5+ 59 ♔xd5 d3 60
♘d6+ ♔b8 61 ♘c4 ♖e4 62 ♔xc5
1-0 Ward-Adams, Hastings Masters
1995.

Points:

Andy	2
Bob	1
Carol	0
Dave	10
Eddy	1

Solution 3-6

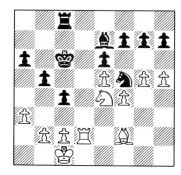

I was present for this awesome
performance of the fantastically
talented young Russian. Rather than
seek a trade he activated his rook
just as **Eddy** would have! The game
went 32...♖h8! 33 ♖d1 h6 34 ♖h1
hxg5 35 ♘xg5 ♗xg5 36 fxg5 ♔d5

37 ♗e1 ♖h7 38 ♗c3 ♔e4 39 b3

cxb3 40 cxb3 ♔f3 41 h6 gxh6 42 gxh6 ♖xh6 43 ♖d1 ♔e4 44 ♖d7 ♖h3 45 ♔b2 ♘e3 46 ♗d2 ♖h2 47 ♔c3 ♘d5+ 48 ♔c2 ♖f2 49 ♖a7 ♔xe5 50 ♖xa6 ♔e4 51 ♖d6 e5 52 a4 ♘e3+ 0-1 Almasi-Morozevich, Birmingham (4NCL) 2000.

Points:

Andy	4
Bob	0
Carol	1
Dave	0
Eddy	10

Solution 3-7

The spectators watching the demonstration boards certainly got their money's worth on this British Championship day. In the 16 ♗d2 lines I'm not sure that Black can't get away with taking the pawn on g2, and I'm awarding the maximum score to **Bob's** 16 g4!? Perhaps Black could have defended better in the game, but White certainly seems to have at least adequate compensation for the exchange:

16...♗xe1 17 ♖xe1 ♖e7 18 g5 ♘d7 19 ♕h5 ♘f8 20 ♖e3 c5 21 d5 g6 22 ♕h6 exd5 23 ♘g4 ♖e6 24 ♘f6+ ♔h8 25 ♖h3 ♖e1+ 26 ♗f1 dxc4

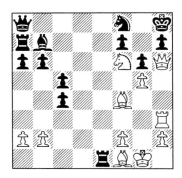

27 ♕xh7+ ♘xh7 28 ♖xh7 mate Emms-Arkell, British Championship 1999.

Points:

Andy	0
Bob	10
Carol	2
Dave	1
Eddy	2

Solution 3-8

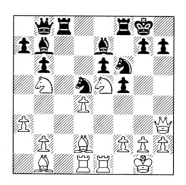

Eddy is absolutely right. Attempts to continue to hit h7 will be fruit-less whereas e6 is now clearly a weak point: 21 ♗a2! a6 22 ♘c3 ♖ce8 23 ♘f3 ♗d8 24 ♘g5 ♕c8 25 ♖xe6!

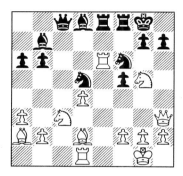

25...♖xe6 26 ♘xd5 h6 27 ♘xf6+ ♔h8 28 ♕xf5 ♖e1+ 29 ♖xe1 ♕xf5 30 ♘f7+ 1-0 Gipslis-Savon, USSR Championship, Baku 1961.

Points:

Andy	0
Bob	1
Carol	0
Dave	1
Eddy	10

Solution 3-9

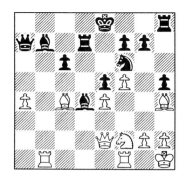

Forget Nostradamus, it's the prophecy of *Eddy* that came true! Next came 26 ♘h3 ♕xa4 27 ♘g5 ♕a8 28 ♘xf7!

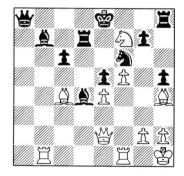

when the tactical point here is that after 28...♖xf7 29 ♗xf7+ ♔xf7 30 ♕c4+, either the white queen would invade on e6 to devastating effect or at the very least the piece would be regained via say 30...♔f8 31 ♕b4+. Hence 28...♖f8 29 ♘g5 c5 30 ♗b5 ♗xe4 31 ♗xd7+ ♔xd7 32 ♘xe4 ♘xe4 33 ♕c4 ♔c7 34 ♕e6 ♖e8 35 ♕f7+ ♔c6 36 ♗e7 ♕c8 37 ♕xg7 ♘f2+ 38 ♖xf2 ♗xf2 39 ♕f6+

♔d5 40 ♕d6+ ♔e4 41 f6 ♕f5 42 ♕c6+ ♔e3 43 ♗xc5+ ♔d2 44 ♖b2+ ♔c3 45 ♗a3+ 1-0 Plaskett-Chandler, Birmingham (4NCL) 2000.

Points:

Andy	4
Bob	0
Carol	1
Dave	0
Eddy	10

Solution 3-10

It's true that Black would still hold a clear edge after 22...♕b5 despite the white king being nearer the centre for the endgame (and the h1-rook able to come out via h3).

However, there are no realistic attacking chances for White and so I'm backing *Carol's* decision to keep the queens on. Besides, how can you argue with the game continuation of 22...♖fd8 23 ♖h3 ♖ac8 24 ♘c3 ♕e6 25 ♖b1 ♘b5

26 ♕c2 ♗xc3 27 bxc3 ♖xc3 0-1 Rozentalis-Sadler, Hastings Premier 1998.

Points:

Andy	3
Bob	3
Carol	10
Dave	0
Eddy	3

Solutions To Test Four

Solution 4-1

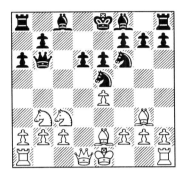

White's straightforward central breakthrough idea was potentially very dangerous. According to Vladimir Kramnik, his selected 10...h5! was an 'intuitive, genuinely Sicilian, strong' move. White deterred from a swift f2-f4 and e4-e5 plan (note 10...g5 11 h4! would have been awkward) and although the rest of the game isn't exactly smooth, many top players, myself and **Andy**(!) stand by his decision: 11 h3 ♕c7 12 f4 ♘c4 13 ♗xc4 ♕xc4 14 ♕f3 h4 15 ♗h2 ♗d7 16 0-0-0 ♖c8 17 ♖he1 b5

(see following diagram)

18 ♕f2 ♕c7 19 e5 b4 20 ♖d3 dxe5 21 fxe5 bxc3 22 ♖xc3 ♕xc3 (cer-

tainly visual although apparently 22...♕b8! would have been stronger) 23 bxc3 ♗a3+ 24 ♔d2 ♘d5 25 ♖e4 ♖xc3 26 ♖g4 0-0 27 ♕xh4 ♖fc8 28 ♘d4 ♗b4 29 ♔e2 ♗b5+ 30 ♘xb5 ♖xc2+ 31 ♔f3 axb5 32 ♖xb4 ♘xb4 33 ♕xb4 ♖8c3+ 0-1 Ivanchuk-Kramnik, Linares 1993.

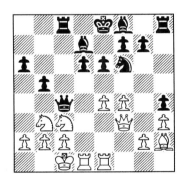

Points:

Andy	10
Bob	1
Carol	3
Dave	1
Eddy	1

Solution 4-2

There are several sensible suggestions here but full points go to the immediate exploitation of Black's light-squared holes and specifically the one on e6.

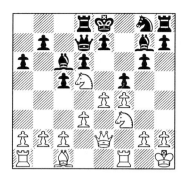

Points:

Andy	1
Bob	10
Carol	1
Dave	2
Eddy	2

Solution 4-3

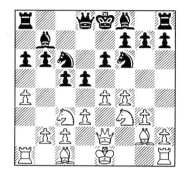

Indeed after 12 ♘g5! Grandmaster Jim Plaskett implied that his opponent probably already had a lost position. His view certainly seems justified by the game continuation: 12...♘f6 13 ♘b6 ♕c7 14 ♘c4 fxe4 15 ♘e6 ♕c8 16 f5

16...♖g8 17 ♘b6 exd3 18 cxd3 ♕b8 19 fxg6 ♗h8 20 g7 ♗xg7 21 ♗g5 ♗h8 22 ♖ae1 ♖d7 23 ♖xf6 exf6 24 ♘xc5+ ♔d8 25 ♘cxd7 ♗xd7 26 ♕e7+ ♔c7 27 ♘d5+ 1-0 Plaskett-Shipov, Hastings Premier 1999. It's **Bob's** selection that gets the point.

At first glance the position seems finely balanced with arguably White's kingside offensive plan being the easier to implement. However, at this specific point in the game, *Dave* is quite right as 9...♘d4! is very awkward: 10 ♘xd4 cxd4 11 ♘d1 dxe4 12 dxe4 ♗b4+ 13 ♗d2 ♗xd2+ 14 ♔xd2, when the white king has been embarrassed and he is left with a bad bishop and a worse pawn structure too. Black should really have racked up the point much sooner than he did: 14...0-0 15 ♘f2 e5 16 f5 a5

(see following diagram)

17 ♖hc1 ♗a6 18 ♘d3 ♘d7 19 ♗f1 ♘c5 20 ♕f3 ♕g5+ 21 ♔e1 ♗xd3 22

♗xd3 ♖ac8 23 ♖d1 ♖c7 24 ♕e2 g6
25 fxg6 fxg6 26 ♗c4+ ♔g7 27 ♗d5
♘d7 28 ♖a3 ♘f6 29 ♖f3 ♘xd5 30
♖xf8 ♘e3 31 ♕f3 ♘xc2+ 32 ♔f2
♕e3+ 33 ♔g2 ♕xf3+ 34 ♖xf3 ♘e3+
35 ♖xe3 dxe3 36 ♔f3 ♖c2 37 ♖d7+
♔h6 38 ♔xe3 ♖xh2 39 ♖e7 ♖xb2
40 ♖xe5 ♖b4 41 ♖e6 ♔g5 42 ♖e7
♖xa4 43 ♖xh7 ♖a3+ 44 ♔d4 ♖xg3
45 ♔d5 a4 46 e5 b5 47 ♖b7 ♖b3
48 e6 a3 49 ♔d6 a2 50 ♖a7 ♖d3+
51 ♔c5 ♖e3 52 ♔d6 ♖e2 53 e7 ♔f6
54 ♖xa2 ♖e6+ 55 ♔c5 g5 56 ♖f2+
♔g6 57 ♔xb5 ♖xe7 58 ♔c4 ♖d7 59
♔c3 g4 60 ♖f4 ♔g5 61 ♖f8 g3 62
♖g8+ ♔f4 63 ♖f8+ ♔e3 64 ♖e8+
♔f2 65 ♖f8+ ♔g1 66 ♖g8 g2 67
♖h8 ♖f7 0-1 Hawes-Ward, Jersey
Open 2000.

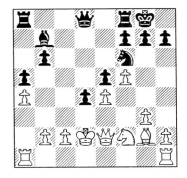

Points:

Andy	1
Bob	1
Carol	2
Dave	10
Eddy	2

Solution 4-4

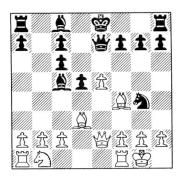

Andy's idea would drop the c7-pawn but after 10...g5! 11 ♗g3 h5!, 12 h3 may lose White a pawn after 12...h4 13 ♗h2 ♘xh2 14 ♔xh2 ♗d4. **Bob** clearly has the best solution and one practical encounter continued 12 ♗a6 ♗xa6 13 ♕xa6 ♗b6 14 ♕a4 ♕e6 15 h4 0-0-0 16 ♘d2 gxh4 17 ♗xh4 ♖dg8 18 ♕f4 ♘xe5 19 ♖fe1 ♘g6 20 ♖xe6 ♘xf4 21 ♖f6 ♘xg2 0-1 Brochet-Hebden, French Team Championship 1998.

Points:

Andy	0
Bob	10
Carol	2
Dave	0
Eddy	1

Solution 4-5
I have a great deal of sympathy for Eddy's view. Needing to win this game to clinch first place in the tournament I gave serious consideration to 17 ♖ad1, 17 ♖fe1 and 17 f4.

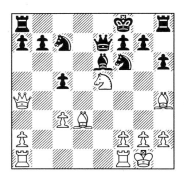

However, I'm very glad that in the end after much consideration I opted for 17 ♖ae1! Indeed *Andy* was quite right as White was then well placed to meet: 17...g5 18 ♗g3 ♘fd5 with 19 f4! gxf4 20 ♗xf4 ♘xf4 21 ♕xf4 ♔e8

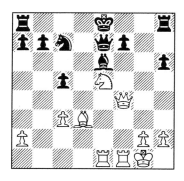

22 ♘xf7! ♔d7 23 ♘e5+ 1-0 Ward-Gligoric, Malta 2000.

Points:

Andy	10
Bob	0
Carol	5
Dave	1
Eddy	5

Solution 4-6

After nearly seven hours of gruelling play a hard-fought game of mine ended 70 ♔c6 ♔f3 71 ♔d5 g4 72 ♖f6+ ♔e3 73 ♖g6 ♔f3 74 ♔d4 g3 75 ♔d3 g2 76 ♔d2 ♔f2 77 ♖f6+ ♔g3 78 ♖g6+ ♔f2 79 ♖xg2+ ♔xg2 ½-½ McDonald-Ward, Millennium Masters, Oakham 2000. Indeed the black king did prevent its enemy number from returning to thwart the pawn. With this in mind things could have been so different if *Dave's* advice had been followed: 70 ♖f6!! ♔h3 71 ♔c6 g4 72 ♔d5 g3 73 ♔e4 g2 74 ♔f3 g1♘+

75 ♔f2 ♔h2 76 ♖h6+ ♘h3+ 77
♔f3. The knight drops next and
mate follows.

Points:

Andy	2
Bob	0
Carol	2
Dave	10
Eddy	1

Solution 4-7

Not for the first time there is a
certain appeal to Bob's way of
thinking. You can see why he enjoys
his chess so much. Nevertheless, it
seems unnecessary to go for broke
now when a simple chiselling plan so
readily suggests itself. White
chose **Eddy's** plan: 16 h4! bxc3 17
bxc3 ♔h8 18 h5 gxh5 19 ♕h3 h4 20
exd6 cxd6 21 f5! d5 22 f6

(see following diagram)

22...♘xf6 23 ♘xf6 ♗xf6 24 ♘f4
♖d6 25 ♗c2 ♖g8 26 ♘h5 ♗g5 27
♕d3 f6 28 ♘xf6 ♗xf6 29 ♖xf6
♕g7 30 ♕f3 ♖c6 31 ♖f7 ♖xc3 32
♖xg7 ♖xf3 33 ♖h7 mate Hodgson-

Rowson, Oxford 1998.

Points:

Andy	1
Bob	5
Carol	1
Dave	0
Eddy	10

Solution 4-8

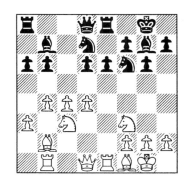

Andy's idea is nice in theory, but
fails in practice. After 17 d5 exd5
18 ♖xe8+ ♕xe8 19 cxd5, 19...b5 is
awkward, facilitating ...♘b6 attacking the d-pawn. I am a great fan of
Matthew Sadler and that is why
Carol hits the mark for me: 17

♘d2. Her plan is straightforward and would certainly be successful. Black has nothing to attack on the kingside and that explains the game continuation: 17...d5 18 c5 bxc5 19 bxc5 ♕c7 20 ♘a2 ♗c6 21 ♘b4 ♗b5 22 ♗xb5 axb5 23 ♕e2 ♗h6 24 ♖bd1 ♖eb8 25 ♘b1 ♘h5 26 ♘c3 ♖a5 27 ♘cxd5 exd5 28 ♘xd5 ♕d8 29 ♘e7+ ♔f8 30 ♘c6

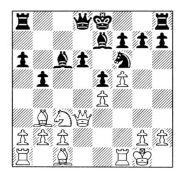

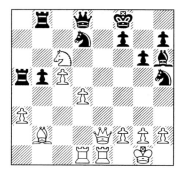

30...♘f4 31 ♕g4 ♕c7 32 ♘xa5 1-0 Sadler-Korchnoi, Arnhem 1999.

Points:

Andy	2
Bob	0
Carol	10
Dave	1
Eddy	1

Solution 4-9

A simple but very effective technique was now demonstrated by the player many consider as the best ever. A g2-g4-g5 policy if successful would certainly cramp Black, but easier still is the no-risk policy of *Eddy*.

His suggested method of progression offers Black no opportunity to get in the thematic ...d6-d5 break: 13 ♗g5 ♕b6+ 14 ♔h1 0-0 15 ♗xf6 ♗xf6 16 ♗d5 ♖ac8 17 ♗xc6 ♖xc6 18 ♖ad1 ♖fc8 19 ♘d5 ♕d8 20 c3 ♗e7 21 ♖a1 f6 22 a4

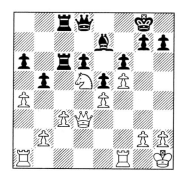

22...♖b8 23 ♘xe7+ 1-0 Fischer-Gadia, Mar del Plata 1960. Eddy's dream came true(!), the point being as well that it's really a knight rather than a queen that White desires on d5.

Points:

Andy	2
Bob	2
Carol	2
Dave	1
Eddy	10

Solution 4-10

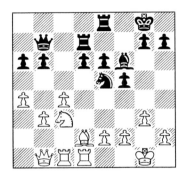

There were actually some reasonable suggestions from our panel here (did you expect otherwise?), but by far the most astute was **Bob's**. Often lunging out in the following manner can be detrimental, but such kingside expansion is justified here with all of White's army lying dormant on the queenside: 22...g5! 23 ♗e3 h5 24 ♗d4 h4 25 ♗xe5 ♗xe5 26 g4 h3! 27 f3 ♖g7! 28 e4 fxg4 29 fxg4 ♖f8 30 ♖d3 ♖f4 31 ♖xh3 ♖xg4+ 32 ♔h1 ♖h7 33 ♕d3 ♖gh4 34 ♖xh4 ♖xh4 35 h3 g4 36 ♖g1 ♕h7

0-1 Agdestein-Adams, European Cup, Slough 1997.

Points:

Andy	0
Bob	10
Carol	2
Dave	2
Eddy	1

Solutions To Test Five

Solution 5-1

It's important to note that ♘g5-e4 is a threat. It's worth Black's while occupying d5 and the knight is the best man for the job. All in all it's as though **Carol** had read the script! The game continued 19...h6! 20 ♖c1 ♘c7 21 ♖dc2 ♘d5 22 g3 ♖ac8 23 ♕d3 ♖xc2 24 ♖xc2 b5

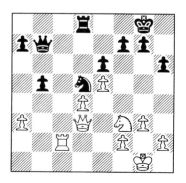

25 ♖c5 a6 26 ♕e4 b4 27 axb4 ♕xb4 28 ♕e1 ♕b3 29 ♔g2 ♖b8 30 ♕c1 ♔h7 31 h4 ♖a8 32 ♖a5 ♕b7 33 h5 ♔g8 34 ♕c2 ♖c8 35 ♖c5 ♖b8 36 ♕c4 ♕a8 37 ♖a5 ♘e3+ 38 fxe3 ♖b2+ 0-1 Gulko-Adams, Internet (rapidplay) 2000.

Points:

Andy	0
Bob	0
Carol	10
Dave	2
Eddy	2

Solution 5-2

The flaw in Bob's logic is that after 22 fxg7, Black intends 22...♖xa3! when a perpetual check will result. Indeed the only continuation that wins for White (and rather quickly too!) is 22 ♔b1! ♖xc2 23 ♖d2!

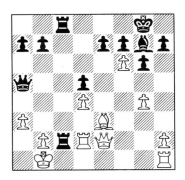

1-0 Hebden-Nunn, Hastings Premier 1998. Thanks to 23...♖xd2 24 ♗xd2! White will net the piece safely and hence maximum score goes to **Dave**.

Points:

Andy	0
Bob	1
Carol	1
Dave	10
Eddy	0

Solution 5-3

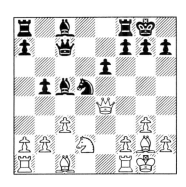

I don't fancy Dave's pawn winning

strategy too much! After 14 ♕d3 a6 15 ♗xd5 exd5 16 ♕xd5 ♗b7 I don't think that I would be going over the top in suggesting that Black would have adequate compensation and besides 15...♖d8 is bad for White too. Eddy has also got a bit confused as the immediate 14 c4 is hardly the way to budge the well placed black knight. Carol's suggestion is reasonable, but it's **Andy** who gets the point. His suggestion creates a long-term weakness which lasted throughout the following game: 14 a4 bxa4 15 ♕xa4 ♗d7 16 ♕c2 ♖ac8 17 ♘e4 ♗b6 18 ♘g5 ♘f6 19 ♖e1 h6 20 ♗f4 ♕c5 21 ♗e3 ♕c7 22 ♘e4 ♘d5 23 ♗xb6 axb6 24 ♕b3 ♖fd8 25 ♖ec1 ♗c6 26 ♖d1 ♘e7 27 ♖xd8+ ♖xd8 28 ♖d1 ♖xd1+ 29 ♕xd1 ♘f5 30 ♕d3 ♗d5 31 ♘f6+ gxf6 32 ♗xd5 ♕e5 33 ♗e4 ♘d6 34 ♗f3 (through simple chess White has emerged with a bishop for a knight and a potentially dangerous queenside majority)

34...f5 35 ♔g2 f4 36 ♕a6 fxg3 37 hxg3 ♕c5 38 b4 ♕c7 39 ♕d3 ♔g7

40 ♕d4+ f6 41 ♕e3 ♔f7 42 ♗g4
♘f5 43 ♗xf5 exf5 44 b5 ♕b7+ 45
♔g1 ♕c7 46 ♕xh6 ♕xc3 47 ♕h5+
♔e6 48 ♕e8+ ♔d6 49 ♕d8+ ♔c5
50 ♕c7+ ♔b4 51 ♕xb6 ♕e1+ 52
♔h2 ♕d2 53 ♔h3 ♕d5 54 ♕c6
♕xb5 55 ♕xf6 ♕f1+ 56 ♔h4 ♕xf2
57 ♕d6+ ♔c3 58 ♔g5 ♕f1 59 ♕e5+
♔b3 60 ♕xf5 ♕g2 61 ♕d3+ ♔a2 62
g4 ♕c6 63 ♕d4 ♕e6 64 ♔f4 ♕h6+
65 ♔g3 ♕g5 66 ♕f4 ♕d5 67 ♕f2+
♔a1 68 ♕f1+ 1-0 Nunn-Tisdall, San
Francisco 1995.

Points:

Andy	10
Bob	2
Carol	3
Dave	0
Eddy	1

Solution 5-4

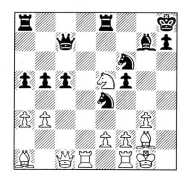

I don't think so, Bob! Your knight on
e5 is en prise. Carol and Eddy have
sensible suggestions, but it's **Andy**
who correctly gets straight to the
point: 26 ♕f4! ♕c8 27 ♘f7+ ♔g8
28 ♘h6+ ♗xh6 29 ♕xh6

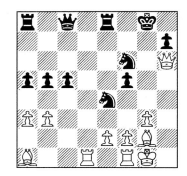

Now the bishop pair on an open
board proves to be too much for
Black to deal with: 29...♔f7 30
♗xe4 ♘xe4 31 ♕xh7+ ♔e6 32
♕g6+ ♔e7 33 ♕g7+ ♔e6 34 f3 1-0
Speelman-Garcia Ilundain, European
Team Championship, Pula 1997.

Points:

Andy	10
Bob	0
Carol	2
Dave	0
Eddy	2

Solution 5-5

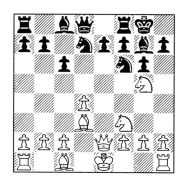

Frankly it's difficult to argue with **Bob** once you've had the pleasure of witnessing the following game continuation: 9 h4!? h6 10 h5! ♘xh5 11 g4 ♘hf6 12 ♘e6!

12...fxe6 13 ♕xe6+ ♖f7 14 ♗xg6 ♕f8 15 g5 ♘d5 16 gxh6 ♘e5 17 ♗h7+! 1-0 W.Watson-Meduna, Prague 1992.

Points:

Andy	3
Bob	10
Carol	2
Dave	2
Eddy	2

Solution 5-6

This was not a trick question and the simplest course of action is clearly the best. As **Eddy** instructed, Black should pressurise the c2-pawn and with ...b7-b5 as well as ...♗xc4 always available to budge the knight, Black's position should practically play itself!

The game continued 18...♖ac8 19 0-0 ♖c6 20 ♖fc1 ♖fc8 21 ♘a5 ♖6c7 22 ♕d2 ♕f4 23 ♕xf4 exf4

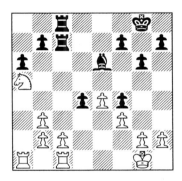

24 c3 b5 25 c4 bxc4 26 bxc4 ♗xc4 27 ♖xc4 ♖xc4 28 ♘xc4 ♖xc4 29 ♖xa6 ♖c1+ 30 ♔f2 ♖c2+ 31 ♔f1 ♖xb2 32 ♖d6 ♖d2 33 ♖f6 d3 34 ♖xf4 ♖a2 35 ♔e1 ♖e2+ 36 ♔d1 ♖xg2 37 h4 ♔g7 38 e5 ♖e2 39 ♖d4 ♖xe5 40 ♖xd3 ♔f5 41 ♔e2 ♖f4 42 h5 g5 43 ♖d5 ♔h6 0-1 El-Kher-Ward, Copenhagen 1998.

Points:

Andy	1
Bob	1
Carol	1
Dave	3
Eddy	10

Solution 5-7

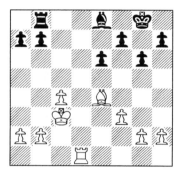

The young Russian Peter Svidler adopted **Carol's** key move here and the rest went according to plan too! 22 f4! ♔f8 23 b4 ♔e7 24 b5 b6 25 a4 ♖c8 26 ♔b3 h6 27 a5 f5 28 ♗f3 g5 29 g3 ♖c5 30 ♔b4 e5 31 fxe5 ♖xe5 32 axb6 axb6 33 ♗d5 ♖e2 34 ♖a1 ♖b2+ 35 ♔c3 ♖xh2 36 ♖a6

Black can create his own passed pawns, but White's are further advanced and more important still, connected: 36...f4 37 gxf4 ♔d6 38 ♖xb6+ ♔c5 39 ♖b8 ♖h3+ 40 ♔d2 ♗g6 41 b6 ♖h2+ 42 ♔e1 ♖b2 43 b7 ♖b1+ 44 ♔d2 ♔d4 45 ♖d8 ♖b2+ 46 ♔e1 ♖b1+ 47 ♔f2 ♖b2+ 48 ♔g1 ♖b1+ 49 ♔h2 1-0 Svidler-Lutz, Frankfurt 1999.

Points:

Andy	3
Bob	1
Carol	10
Dave	1
Eddy	2

Solution 5-8

The problem with Eddy's far from ridiculous idea is that it may ultimately donate Black with a handy outpost on d5. There is no need to give Black any play and following **Bob's** treatment; he certainly doesn't get any! 15 f4! ♗e6 16 h4! fxg4 17 h5 ♗f5 18 hxg6 hxg6 19 ♖h6 ♘c4 20 ♗xf5 gxf5 21 ♖h8+!

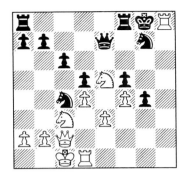

21...♔xh8 22 ♘g6+ ♔g8 23 ♘xe7+ ♔f7 24 ♘xf5 ♔g8 25 ♘h6+ 1-0 Hillarp Persson-Ellen, Recklinghausen Open 1999.

Points:

Andy	0
Bob	10
Carol	2
Dave	0
Eddy	2

Solution 5-9

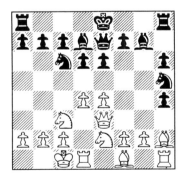

I'm not sure that White wants to allow the black c6-knight to come to e5 as it looks quite good there.

Also as in the game White must watch for Black's ...e6-e5 break (if the white knight ventures from e2). In the text encounter White had a strong solution to this, having previously followed *Carol's* advice: 13 ♗g1!? 0-0-0 14 g4 ♘f6 15 f3 ♘h7 16 ♗f2 e5 17 d5 ♘d4 18 ♘xd4 exd4 19 ♖xd4! ♗xd4 20 ♕xd4

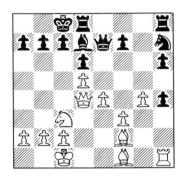

20...b6 21 ♘b5 ♔b7 22 ♕c3 ♖c8 23 ♘d4 ♕f6 24 ♕d3 ♔a8 25 ♗xh4 ♕f4+ 26 ♔b1 ♘f8 27 ♕c3 ♘g6 28 ♗a6 ♘xh4 29 ♗xc8 ♖xc8 30 ♖xh4 ♔b7 31 a3 ♖g8 32 ♘e2 ♕g5 33 ♖h5 ♕e7 34 ♖xh6 f5 35 gxf5 ♗xf5 36 ♘d4 ♗d7 37 ♘e6 ♗c8 38 f4 ♖g4 39 ♕c6+ ♔b8 40 ♖h8 1-0 Leko-Topalov, Frankfurt 1999.

Points:

Andy	2
Bob	1
Carol	10
Dave	1
Eddy	2

Solution 5-10

Yes, you've guessed it, whilst Carol and Eddy have characteristically suggested cautious and steady (not unreasonable) plans, it's **Bob** who gets the last word (for now anyway): 13 ♘g5! ♖d8 14 ♘d5!!, unleashing the b2-bishop, is quite stunning:

(see following diagram)

14...exd5 15 ♗xf6 ♗xf6 16 ♕xh7+ ♔f8 17 cxd5 d6 18 ♗h5 ♗xg5 19 ♕h8+ ♔e7 20 ♕xg7 ♖f8 21 ♕xg5+

♔e8 22 ♖c1 ♕d8 23 ♕f5 ♕e7 24 ♖c4 ♘d7 25 ♖c7 ♗c8 26 ♖fc1 ♔d8 27 ♗g4 ♕e8 28 ♖1c6 ♖g8 29 h3 b5 30 ♕f4 ♕f8 31 ♗xd7 ♗xd7 32 ♕f6+ ♔e8 33 ♖xd6 ♖d8 34 ♖dxd7 1-0 Kiriakov-Tiviakov, Isle Of Man Open 1999.

Points:

Andy	0
Bob	10
Carol	3
Dave	2
Eddy	3

Marking Scheme and Scorechart

	Test 1	Test 2	Test 3	Test 4	Test 5
1					
2					
3					
4					
5					
6					
7					
8					
9					
10					
Total					

0-20 (on each test): You are a lousy guesser. It's back to the drawing board for you, I'm afraid!

21-40: Not too bad, but a bit of work on your chess wouldn't go amiss!

41-60: Reasonable club standard.

61-80: You either are, or have the potential to become, a strong county player.

81-100: Life is looking rosy on the chess front. If you are not already a titled player then I wouldn't rule it out as a possibility. Indeed with 100% I'd say grandmaster level could be on the horizon.